JUNIOR CERTIFICATE

LESS STRESS MORE SUCCESS

Music Revision

Andrew Purcell

Gill & Macmillan

Gill & Macmillan
Hume Avenue
Park West
Dublin 12
with associated companies throughout the world
www.gillmacmillan.ie

© Andrew Purcell 2011

978 07171 4689 5

Design by Liz White Designs
Artwork by Oxford Designers & Illustrators
Music artwork by Halstan Music Setting
Print origination by Carrigboy Typesetting Services

The paper used in this book is made from the wood pulp of managed forests. For every tree felled, at least one tree is planted, thereby renewing natural resources.

All rights reserved.
No part of this publication may be copied, reproduced or transmitted in any form or by any means without written permission of the publishers or else under the terms of any licence permitting limited copying issued by the Irish Copyright Licensing Agency.

Any links to external websites should not be construed as an endorsement by Gill & Macmillan of the content or view of the linked material.

For permission to reproduce photographs, the author and publisher gratefully acknowledge the following:

© Alamy: 14T, 51, 58B, 101, 129TR; © Corbis: 2, 80, 82, 129TL; © Getty Images: 5, 12T, 12B, 13T, 13B, 14B, 57, 58T, 59, 65, 66T, 66B, 67, 72, 79, 86T, 86CR, 86CL, 86B, 90, 93, 129BL, 133L, 133TR, 133BR, 133C; © Imagefile: 102T; © The Irish Times: 134; © Kobal: 102B; © Lebrecht Music & Arts: 129BR; © Photocall Ireland!: 87; © Rex Features: 84; © TopFoto: 62; Courtesy of Sheelyn Browne: 81

The authors and publisher have made every effort to trace all copyright holders, but if any has been inadvertently overlooked we would be pleased to make the necessary arrangement at the first opportunity.

CONTENTS

- 1. How the Exam is Marked 1
- 2. The Music Practical 2
- 3. Exam Technique 6
- 4. A Quick Guide to Music Theory 8
- 5. Set Songs **EXAM Q.1** 24
- 6. Set Works **EXAM Q.2** 47
- 7. Irish Traditional Music **EXAM Q.3** 82
- 8. Melodic and Rhythmic Dictation **EXAM Q.4** 97
- 9. Choice Songs and Choice Works **EXAM Q.5** 101
- 10. Triads **EXAM Q.6** 109

11. Melody Writing **EXAM Q.7** 113

12. Harmony **EXAM Q.8** 118

13. Free Composition **EXAM Q.9** 126

14. Chosen General Study **EXAM Q.8** OL/ **EXAM Q.10** HL.......129

15. Instruments of the Orchestra and Performing Mediums.......133

16. Structure and Forms of Music..135

Glossary of Musical Terms 137

> **HL** *Note:* Material that is to be studied only by those taking Higher level is indicated in the text.

1 How the Exam is Marked

aims
- To understand the marking scheme and the percentage allocated to each question.

In total there are **400 marks** (100%) for the Junior Certificate Music examination.

The **Practical** (100 marks, or 25% of the total) is usually examined just before or just after the Easter holidays.

The **Written Paper** is worth 300 marks or 75% of the total.

Higher level

Marks per question:

- Question 1 Set Songs – 30 marks (10% of paper).
- Question 2 Set Works – 30 marks (10% of paper).
- Question 3 Irish Music – 40 marks (roughly 13% of paper).
- Question 4 Dictation – 40 marks (roughly 13% of paper).
- Question 5 Choice Songs and Works – 40 marks (roughly 13% of paper).
- Question 6 Triads – 20 marks (roughly 7% of paper).
- Question 7 Melody Writing – 35 marks (roughly 12% of paper).
- Question 8 Harmony – 45 marks (15% of paper).
- Question 9 Original Composition (**instead of Questions 6–8**) – 100 marks (roughly 33% of paper).
- Question 10 Chosen General Study – 20 marks (roughly 7% of paper).

Ordinary level

The Higher and Ordinary level papers are very similar in marking set-up and correction.

In Ordinary level:

- Question 6 is worth 40 marks.
- Question 7 is worth 60 marks (a huge 20% of the written paper).
- Question 8 in Ordinary level is the Chosen General Study (20 marks).
- There is no Harmony question on the Ordinary level paper.

key point

Though the exam paper has remained very similar for many years, it is liable to change at any time as long as it complies with the Junior Certificate music syllabus.

2 The Music Practical

aims
- To become aware of the importance of the practical exam.
- To understand the value of good preparation and rehearsal.

Practice and performance tips

Your performance counts for **25%** of your Junior Certificate Music examination, so you must put in the **practice** it deserves over two or three years. The standard is high and is based on the equivalent of three years of classroom-based activity. So get practising!

- Choose a practice time when you are well rested and your enthusiasm is high. A pleasant atmosphere, undisturbed by noise, will help you concentrate on your practice objectives.
- Try to find a comfortable, quiet place to practise. Good air circulation and good lighting are also very important.
- Performing music is for the ear. You want to sound better. So, above all, remember to listen to yourself as you play or sing. This is difficult, so try to record your playing or singing when practising. Then listen back carefully and decide what you need to do to make your performance better. This habit will improve your listening technique. You will be able to hear and judge your own playing instead of relying on somebody else to do it. By listening to your old recordings, you can hear the improvement you've made.
- Do it right from the very first practice! Always aim for perfection in notes, sound, and musical expression.

- Write things down. You will remember things if you write them down. When you see what you've written a day, two days, or a week later, it refreshes your memory and helps you remember it permanently.
- Create your own style by interpretation. Circle all the dynamics and tempo markings in your pieces. Write in your score how you want the piece to sound, e.g. lively, slow, calm, etc.
- Look at practising as problem solving. Don't look at practising as repeating your pieces a certain number of times. Instead, view it as your time to find and solve problems in your pieces.

key point

Remember the **five times easier** rule: It is five times easier to learn it right the first time than to re-learn it after learning it incorrectly!

The Music Practical examination

exam TIPS

1. First impressions are important.

2. **Look and feel confident** from the moment you walk into the room/hall.

3. Choose to perform pieces that are not too difficult for your ability. Choosing something that you can perform **fluently** and performing it well will build your confidence throughout your performance.

4. You will be nervous, but keep your nerves under control. **Controlled nerves** help you give your best.

5. Don't forget to **breathe**. This applies not only to singers, but all performers!

6. Be so **well prepared** that you can play or sing with comfort and ease. Practise, practise, practise!

7. No matter how you feel you have performed, this element of the exam is not over until you leave the room or hall. Keep your **focus** to the end.

> **key point**
>
> The most important tip is to be **over-prepared**. You should be able to perform the piece in your sleep! If you are over-prepared, you will be as confident as you can possibly be. However, make sure you don't perform your pieces as if you are totally bored with them! All of your pieces must have a musical life about them.

An accompanist should always be provided where an accompaniment is required for the proper realisation of the music being performed.

Junior Certificate Guidelines for Teachers

Performance requirements

Each student gets a maximum time to perform all of his/her pieces. This time includes time taken for the unprepared tests.

Ordinary level – maximum 10 minutes.
Higher level – maximum 15 minutes.

Ordinary level comprises two songs or pieces and one unprepared test.

Higher level candidates may perform:
- four pieces in one activity and one unprepared test; **or**
- two pieces in each of two different activities and one unprepared test.

Pieces should be of a good standard that you can perform well.
- Don't pick something too easy.
- Don't pick something which is beyond your skill level.

You get marks for 'musicality':

1. Accuracy of note playing (**control** – 20 marks).
2. Interpretation of the music (**chosen music and standard of performance** – 60 marks).
3. Unprepared test (20 marks – see notes below).

THE MUSIC PRACTICAL

- Solo and group performing are regarded as separate performing activities.
- Check with your music teacher which instruments can or cannot be presented as two separate activities.
- Accompaniment or duet performance is treated as group performance.
- The same music may not be presented for two different activities.

Unprepared Tests

Unprepared tests are worth **20 marks** or 5% of your overall exam marks. You have to choose **one** of the following:

- sightreading (on instrument or voice).
- aural memory rhythm (clapping back).
- aural memory melody (singing back).
- improvisation.

You can choose to do these aural tests on a different instrument (medium) from the one you have played/sung for your music practical examinations.

Sightreading

Look at the time signature, key signature and tempo indications first. Then quickly look over the music you are about to play. **Keep your place no matter what**, even if it means missing notes and/or rhythms. Go for an overall effect.

Don't be tentative. Play convincingly, like you know what you're doing. Stay calm!

NB: Previous tests are available on the State Examinations Commission website: www.examinations.ie.

3 Exam Technique

aims
- To become familiar with the requirements of the exam.
- To be prepared for exam procedures on the day.

- Use correct **musical terminology** in answering all questions or try to explain as well as you can your thoughts on the answer (example: discuss the *mood* of a piece).
- Do **not** leave any blank spaces in your exam booklet (except Question 9 – Higher level).
- Use more than single-word answers, especially when asked to describe or explain something. Give detailed and relevant information, including musical features that you hear, if needed.
- Use your time off before the music exam effectively.
- Study thoroughly your: set songs; set works; choice songs and works; and Irish music notes.
- Use your textbook, workbook and this revision book and listen to your set songs and set works CD extracts many times so that you gain a full understanding of each type and piece of music.
- **Practise** melody writing and harmony questions from past papers. These are available in bookshops or from the State Examinations Commission website.
- Familiarise yourself with the question types and allocation of marks per question (see beginning of this revision book).

In the exam hall

- Fill in your examination number, read the exam paper and follow all instructions on the paper.
- The first excerpt on the CD will be to make sure that you are able to hear the music perfectly in whatever room or hall you are sitting your exam. If you have a problem hearing the music on the CD, don't be afraid to let the supervisor know, so that it can be fixed.
- **Read each question at least twice.**
- **Highlight the key words in each question.**

EXAM TECHNIQUE

- Note the command word – 'circle', 'describe', 'state', 'explain', 'find', 'suggest', 'list', etc. For example, 'state and describe' means state and then describe fully – in other words you will need to write a few sentences!

- 'Circle' means circle the correct answer/s! Don't confuse the corrector. If you make a mistake, be very clear about which answer you think is correct. For example: 'Circle TWO correct answers' means circle only two. If you circle more, you may be penalised and marks may be taken off your total.

- **Allocate your time carefully.** There is no need to rush, as you have two hours for this exam. If you finish before the two hours are up, don't leave early: go back and make sure you have answered every question fully. Don't leave any blank spaces for the question that asks you to describe something.

- All musical notations you have written should be correct and as neat as possible. Use a sharp B pencil when composing. It is easier to correct mistakes in pencil than in pen!

- Attempt the correct number of questions. You can answer more than one melody (Question 7 a, b or c) and harmony question (Question 8 a, b or c), but it is better to attempt one fully than to give three incomplete or rushed answers!

- Study the given melody and harmony bars in detail (Questions 6–8). For example, sing the given bars in your head a number of times before deciding on any rhythm for your answering phrase.

exam focus

- Past years' exam papers and musical excerpts, marking schemes, Chief Examiner's reports, unprepared tests and any changes in general guidelines are available from www.examinations.ie.

- The Junior Certificate Music syllabus and Guidelines for Teachers are available from www.education.ie (the Department of Education and Science website).

- The PPMTA (Post Primary Music Teachers' Association) runs local workshops and an annual conference for music teachers: www.ppmta.ie.

4 A Quick Guide to Music Theory

aims
- To develop a clear understanding of some of the various aspects of music theory.

Staffs and clefs

A **staff** or **stave** is made up of five horizontal lines and four spaces as shown below:

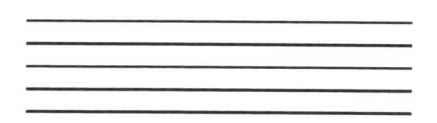

Notes (pitches) are named after the first seven letters of the alphabet: **A B C D E F G**.

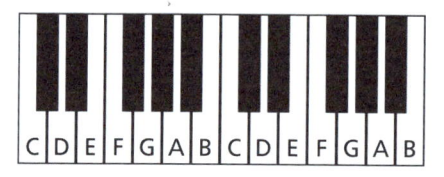

| C | D | E | F | G | A | B | C | D | E | F | G | A | B |

key point
Be able to draw a *virtual piano* and name all the notes!

A **clef** is a musical symbol placed at the beginning of the staff, which establishes the letter names of the lines and spaces.

The two main clefs are the **treble**: 𝄞 and the **bass**: 𝄢

Treble clef notes: e–g–b–d–f (lines), f–a–c–e (spaces), with ledger notes d, e–f–g–a–b–c–d–e–f–g

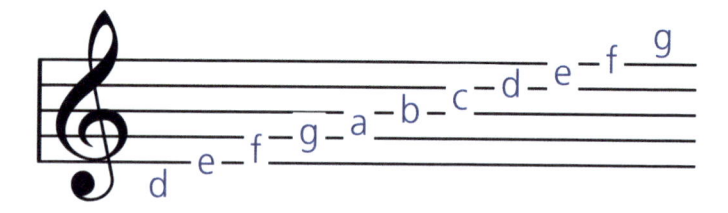

Bass clef notes: g–b–d–f–a (lines), a–c–e–g (spaces), with ledger notes f, g–a–b–c–d–e–f–g–a–b

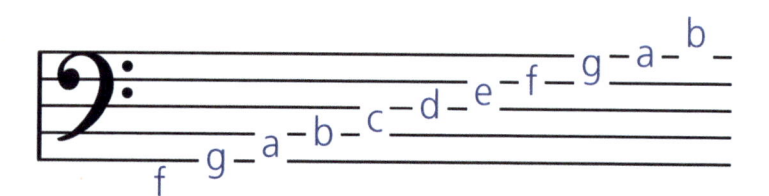

A QUICK GUIDE TO MUSIC THEORY

A **grand staff** or **grand stave** is a combination of both the treble and bass clefs connected by a vertical line on the left side of the staves.

Ledger lines are an extension of the staff. They are additional lines both above and below, which are parallel to the staff. **Each ledger line contains one note.**

Some orchestral instruments use the C clef. In the diagram below, we can see middle C as it is notated in the treble, bass and C clefs.

Note values and rhythms

Each type of note has a specific duration. Time is measured in sound and silence, sound is measured in notes and silence is measured in rests.

Name	Value	Note	Rest
Semibreve (whole note)	4 crotchets		
Minim (half note)	2 crotchets		
Crotchet (quarter note)	1 crotchet		
Quaver (eighth note)	½ of a crotchet		
Semiquaver (sixteenth note)	¼ of a crotchet		
Demisemiquaver (thirty-second note)	⅛ of a crotchet		
Hemidemisemiquaver (sixty-fourth note)	1/16 of a crotchet		

Major and minor

The major scale

A major scale consists of seven different notes.
The intervals from note to note of the major scale in any key are:

tone – tone – semitone – tone – tone – tone – semitone

The C major scale consists of all white keys on the keyboard.

The C major scale is: The G major scale is:

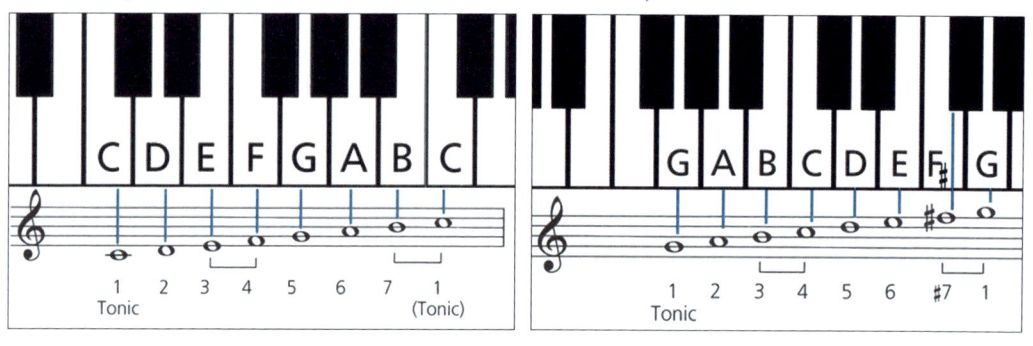

The minor scale (harmonic)

A minor scale consists of seven different notes. The intervals from note to note are:

tone – semitone – tone – tone – semitone – tone and a half – semitone

The C harmonic minor scale is:

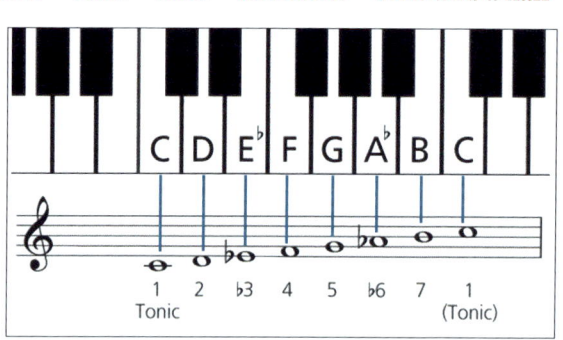

> The key signature for the minor scale is the same as its relative major scale. For example: C major has the same key signature as A minor; G major has the same key signature as E minor.
> Find the major key signature first. Three semitones below this major key note is the relative minor key note.

The C harmonic minor scale is **related** to the E flat major scale, and shares that scale's key signature (three flats).

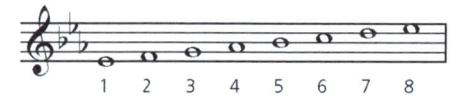

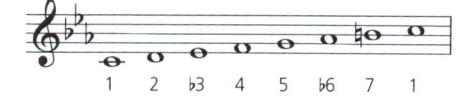

A QUICK GUIDE TO MUSIC THEORY

Understanding musical features

It is very important to have an understanding of **musical analysis** – the **characteristics** of the music.

It is also important to answer questions about the music on your course with the correct musical terms in the Set Songs, Set Works, Choice Songs/Works and Irish Music sections. Here are the terms that you **must** understand.

cadences	instrumental techniques	rhythm/metre
compositional devices	instrumentation	style/genre
dynamics	key signatures	tempo
form	melodic shape	texture
harmony	orchestration	time signature
historical periods	range	tonality

Style/genre

Style describes the typical way composers of different ages write a piece of music and the way it sounds – the way the many musical features of melody, rhythm, harmony, timbre (tone colour), texture, form, tempo, etc. are put together to form a piece of music, whether it is a classical symphony by Mozart or an early twentieth-century ballet by Stravinsky.

What words do you use when asked to describe the 'style' or 'genre' of a given excerpt?

As a music student it is important that you listen to as many different musical styles as possible. When you hear a new piece of music, try to find a suitable stylistic description from the list below.

classical	traditional	absolute music
vocal	blues	fusion
operatic	electronic music	musical theatre
symphonic	ethnic	oriental/eastern
instrumental	country and western	secular
pop/popular	jazz/jazzy	sacred (religious)
rock	programme music	
folk	film music	

Historical periods of classical music: Features

Medieval: c.800–1400

- Monophonic texture – Gregorian chant and modes.
- Later more elaborate polyphonic textures appeared – motets and introduction of harmony.

Renaissance: c.1450–1600

- Rich variety of pieces, both sacred and secular.
- Mainly religious vocal forms but also instrumental dances.
- More complex textures – counterpoint and lots of imitation.
- Use of modes, but major and minor are more prominent.
- Palestrina, Tallis, Thomas Morley.

Baroque: c.1600–1750

Baroque music describes the highly decorative style of classical music from around the early seventeenth century to the death of J. S. Bach in 1750. Music from Germany, Italy and England was most prominent, especially that of Bach, Handel, Vivaldi, Monteverdi and Purcell.

- Major–minor key system instigated.
- Mainly complex polyphonic forms – counterpoint, canon, fugue – with choral music and instrumental dance forms being the most important.
- Only one mood per section or piece and only either loud or soft used (terraced dynamic) per section.
- Lively, fast rhythms with long, ornamented melodies.

Classical: c.1750–1820

- Increase in use of piano and organised orchestra.
- Instrumental music forms (symphony, concerto, sonata, string quartet) develop into structured designs.
- Clear texture (usually homophonic) with melody (short, balanced phrases) most important.
- Mozart, Haydn, Beethoven.

Romantic: c.1820–1900

- Expansion of the orchestra, development of instruments.
- Greater technical virtuosity by instrumentalists.
- Adventurous harmonies with lyrical melodies.
- Greater contrast in textures, dynamics and timbre.
- Programme music – huge symphonic works and operas.
- Chopin, Tchaikovsky, Wagner.

Impressionist: c.1880–1910s

- Modal scales and unusual harmonies.
- Fluid, shifting melodies – no clear-cut structures.
- Colourful orchestral sounds.
- Debussy, Ravel, Fauré.

Modern: c.1900–present

- Huge variety of styles.
- Atonal music (music with no key centre).
- Tonal music (film music/musical theatre).
- Huge mixture of instrumental/vocal ensembles.
- Fusion with popular, folk, jazz and rock music styles.
- Stravinsky, Schoenberg, Bernstein.

Dynamics

Dynamics means the loudness or quietness of a sound. You must understand each dynamic marking in terms of:
- comparison with other dynamics written in the music.
- the dynamic scope for that instrument or ensemble.
- the abilities of the performer(s).

Traditionally, dynamic markings are based on Italian words.

Typical dynamic markings

ppp pp p mp mf f ff fff

p = piano, soft
m = mezzo, moderately
f = forte, loud

If the composer wants the change from one dynamic level to another to be gradual, different markings are added. A ***crescendo*** (***cresc.***) means 'gradually get louder'; a ***decrescendo*** or ***diminuendo*** (***dim.***) means 'gradually get softer'. The markings below also mean *crescendo* and *diminuendo*:

crescendo   diminuendo

exam focus (HL)
You only need to add dynamic marks if you answer Question 9: Free Composition (Higher level only).

key point
As a rule of thumb, each dynamic level, louder or softer than the previous level, should be twice as loud or twice as soft. *ff* should be about twice as loud as *f*.

Articulation

Articulation is **how one sings or plays the notes** of a piece. Exactly how each articulation should be played depends on the instrument playing it, as well as on the style and period of the music.

The main articulations that you should know are:

- **Accents** – an attack to each note.
- **Sforzando (sfz)** are accents which are usually stronger and longer, and more likely to be used in a long note that starts loudly and then suddenly gets much softer or vice versa.
- **Staccato** – short, detached notes. This is shown with a dot under or over the note.
- **Marcato** – stressed, accented notes.
- **Legato** – the opposite of staccato. Smooth, connected series of notes (varies in string or wind playing).
- **Slur** – only the first note of a set of slurred notes has a definite articulation. All other notes under the slur are played legato.

key point: Don't get slurs and ties mixed up!

exam focus

Phrase marks are needed for Question 7, Melody Writing. Don't forget to insert a phrase mark for the four bars that you complete or for the entire melody if asked (Question 7c).

Tempo

The tempo of a piece of music is the **speed** at which it is played.

There are two ways to specify a tempo.

- **Metronome markings** are fixed and exact. They are given in beats per minute.
- **Verbal descriptions** of speed are more personal, depending on the performer.

Tempo instructions are usually given in Italian. The common **tempo markings** that you need to know are:

- *Grave* – very slow and solemn.
- *Largo* – slow and broad.
- *Adagio* – slow.
- *Lento* – slow.
- *Andante* – at a walking pace, a medium–slow tempo.
- *Moderato* – moderate, or medium.
- *Allegretto* – not as fast as allegro.
- *Allegro* – fast.
- *Vivo* or *Vivace* – lively and brisk.
- *Presto* – very fast.
- *Prestissimo* – very, very fast.

More useful Italian terms:

- *poco* – a little.
- *molto* – a lot.
- *più* – more.
- *meno* – less.
- *mosso* – literally 'moved'; movement.
- *rallentando (rall.)* or *ritardando (rit.)* – slowing down.
- *accelerando (accel.)* – speeding up.

Texture

Terms that describe **texture**:

- dense/rich.
- thin/sparse.
- monophonic.
- homophonic.
- polyphonic.
- counterpoint or contrapuntal.
- countermelody or descant.
- canon or canonic.
- fugue.
- antiphonal.

When you describe the **texture** of a piece of music, you are describing how much is going on in the music at any given moment. For example, the texture of a piece of music may have many **layers** or just one or two. It might be made up of rhythm alone; of a melody line with chordal accompaniment; or of many interweaving melodies.

- **Monophonic** music has only one melodic line, with no harmony. Example: plainchant.
- **Homophonic** music has one clear melody line and this is the most important line. All other parts provide some type of accompaniment to the melody. Example: ballad-type song.
- **Polyphonic** music can also be called counterpoint or contrapuntal music. There are two or more independent melody lines being performed at once. Example: a canon/round. Music that is mostly homophonic can become temporarily polyphonic if an independent countermelody is added. Example: the last verse of a Christmas carol with descant part for sopranos.

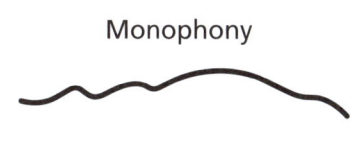

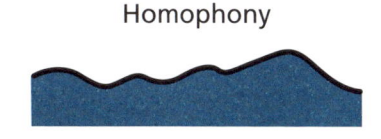

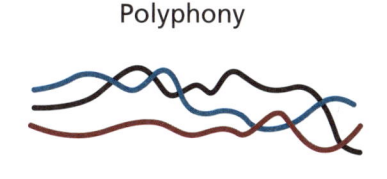

Monophony

Homophony

Polyphony

Harmonic analysis

Harmonic analysis just means understanding how a chord is related to the key and to the other chords in a piece of music.

- **Harmonic rhythm** refers to how often the chords change.
- **Diatonic** harmony stays in a particular major or minor key.
- **Chromatic** harmony includes notes and chords that are not in the key, so it contains many accidentals.
- **Dissonance** means a note, chord or interval that does not fit into the triadic harmonies. A dissonance may sound surprising, jarring, even disagreeable.

Accompaniment

All parts of the music that are not melody are part of the accompaniment. This includes rhythmic parts, harmonies, the bass line and chords.

- **Bass line** – this means the lowest notes that are being sung or played. The bass line also often outlines the chord progression (Question 8a).
- **Inner voices** (Question 8b (SATB)) are accompaniment parts that fill in the music between the melody (often the highest part) and the bass line.
- **Descant** – the melody is not always the highest line in the music. Attention is naturally drawn to high notes, so a part that is higher than the melody is sometimes given a special name such as 'descant'.

Intervals

The distance between two pitches is the **interval** between them. The name of an interval depends both on how the notes are written and on the actual distance between the notes as measured in **semitones**.

The first step in naming the interval is to find the distance between the notes *as they are written on the staff*. The interval between G and C is a fourth (G, A, B, C). The interval between F and E is a seventh. **Compound intervals** are larger than an octave.

Perfect intervals

Unison, octaves, fourths, and fifths can be perfect intervals:

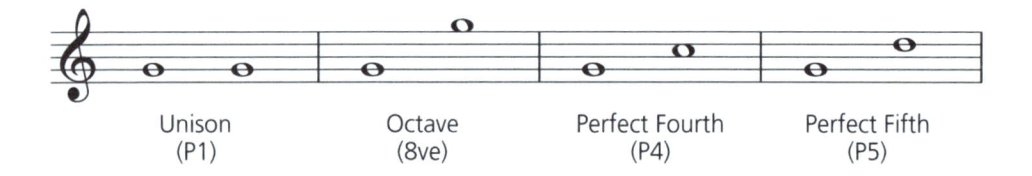

Unison (P1)   Octave (8ve)   Perfect Fourth (P4)   Perfect Fifth (P5)

A QUICK GUIDE TO MUSIC THEORY

Major and minor intervals

Seconds, thirds, sixths and sevenths can be major intervals or minor intervals. The minor interval is always a semitone smaller than the major interval.

1 semitone = minor second (m2)	9 semitones = major sixth (M6)
2 semitones = major second (M2)	10 semitones = minor seventh (m7)
3 semitones = minor third (m3)	11 semitones = major seventh (M7)
4 semitones = major third (M3)	12 semitones = perfect octave (P8)
8 semitones= minor sixth (m6)	

Minor Second (m2)   Major Second (M2)   Minor Third (m3)   Major Third (M3)

Minor Sixth (m6)   Major Sixth (M6)   Minor Seventh (m7)   Major Seventh (M7)

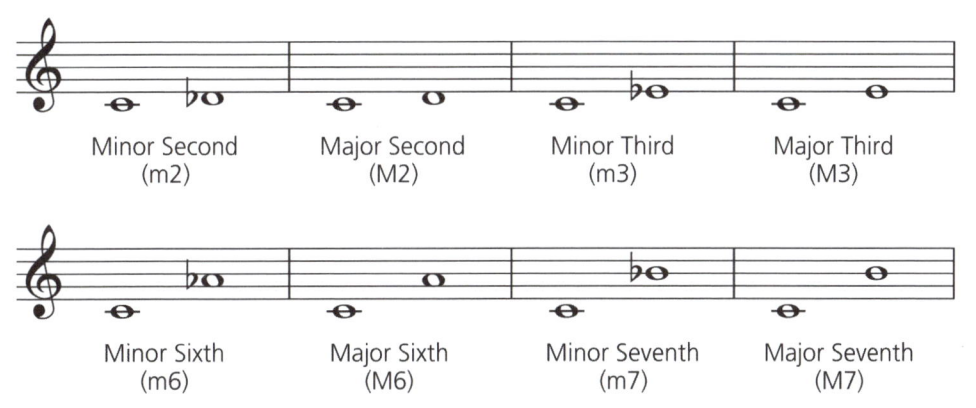

Intervals – consonance and dissonance

Notes that sound good together when played at the same time are called **consonant** or **concord** sounds. Notes that are **dissonant** can sound harsh or unpleasant when played at the same time (**discordant**).

The intervals considered to be **consonant** are the minor third, major third, perfect fourth, perfect fifth, minor sixth, major sixth and the octave.

The intervals considered to be **dissonant** are the minor second, major second, minor seventh, major seventh and, particularly, the **tritone** (example: C–F#).

Rhythm

- The term **rhythm** can mean the basic pulse of the music or a rhythmic pattern that is repeated throughout the music. It can also refer to the pattern of note values.
- The **beat** is the steady pulse in the music. Anything that happens at the same time as a strong pulse is 'on the beat'. Anything that happens 'off the beat' is called **syncopation**. Syncopation occurs when a strong note happens either on a weak beat or off the beat.
- Beats are grouped into **bars**. The first beat is usually the strongest. This sets up a basic rhythm in the pulse of the music.

Words to describe rhythmic features in a Listening Question:

- syncopated.
- dotted.
- complex.
- simple.
- strict/steady.
- ostinato.
- waltz-like.
- triplet.
- free rhythm.
- rubato.
- back beat.

Metre and time signatures

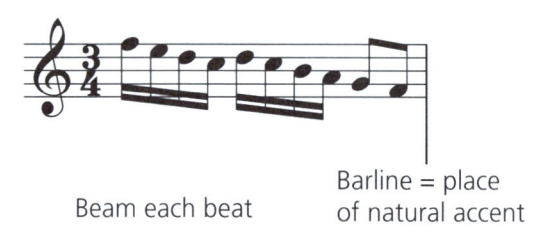

Beam each beat

Barline = place of natural accent

The **metre** is the pulse or beat of the music in each bar.

The **time signature** is indicated by a fraction and is located at the beginning of a piece of music. The lower number tells us what kind of note value receives one beat. The upper number tells us how many beats are in a bar.

In **simple** time the upper number is 2, 3 or 4. Each beat can be subdivided by **two**. In **compound** time the upper number is 6, 9 or 12. Each beat is a **dotted note** (dotted crotchet = 1½ beats) and can be subdivided into groups of **three beats**.

exam focus

The **time signature** appears at the beginning of a piece of music, after the key signature. You only need to insert one time signature in **Question 7a or Question 7c – Melody Writing**. Unlike the key signature, **do not** insert the time signature at the start of each stave or phrase (unless you are changing time signature – which there is no need for you to do).

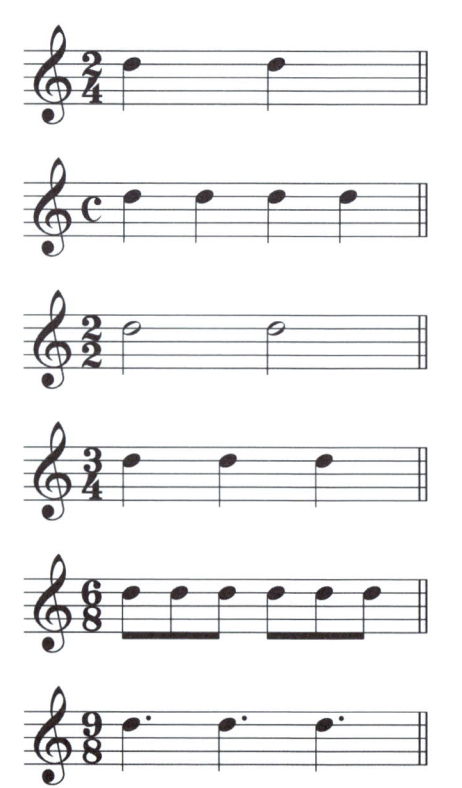

Beats and measures
In most music, things tend to happen right at the beginning of each bar. This is called being on the **downbeat**.

4/4 time is used so often that it is referred to as **common time**, written as a C.

Dotted notes
A **dot** placed to the immediate right of the note-head increases its time value by half; so a minim (half note) followed by a dot is equivalent to three crotchets. Dots after rests increase their time-value in the same way as dots after notes.

Beams and beaming
When notes with flags/tails lie together in groups they are often linked by one or more lines called **beams**. A group of two quavers first unbeamed and then beamed looks like this:

Tied notes
A **tie** joins two or more notes of the same pitch. The first pitch is sung or played and held for the duration of the notes affected by the tie. Note that the tie is always written so as to join the note-heads of two notes. The tie is placed between the note-heads (without touching them). Remember: rests are never tied!

Key signatures
The key signature at the beginning of a musical stave lists the sharps or flats in the key. The key signature comes right after the clef symbol on the stave/staff. It may have some sharp symbols or some flat symbols on particular lines or spaces. If there are no flats or sharps listed after the clef symbol, the key signature is all natural notes (white notes on the piano).
The key signature is a list of all the sharps and flats in the key that the music is in.
The sharps or flats always appear in the same order in all key signatures.
The clef and the key signature are the only symbols that must appear on every staff.

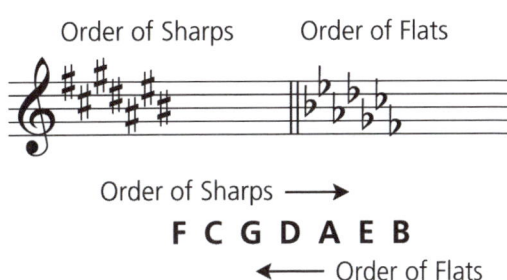

exam focus
You must know every major and minor key up to two sharps and two flats for Junior Certificate!

Order of Sharps   Order of Flats

Order of Sharps ⟶
F C G D A E B
⟵ Order of Flats

LESS STRESS MORE SUCCESS

> **key point**
>
> An easy way to remember the order of sharps is:
> **F**ather **C**harles **G**oes **D**own **A**nd **E**nds **B**attle.
>
> The order of flats is the same sentence in reverse:
> **B**attle **E**nds **A**nd **D**own **G**oes **C**harles's **F**ather.

In the diagram of key signatures on p. 21 you will see that sharps and flats are always added in the same order in which keys get sharper or flatter.

Important hint

If you do not know what key you are in, the key signature can help you to find out.

If you are in a **major key** and if the key contains sharps, the name of the key (doh or tonic key) is one semitone higher than the last sharp in the key signature.

If the key contains flats, the name of the key signature (doh or tonic key) is the name of the **second-to-last flat** in the key signature (don't forget to add the **flat** after the note name).

The only major keys that these rules do **not** work for are C major (no flats or sharps) and F major (one flat). It is easiest just to memorise the key signatures for these two very common keys.

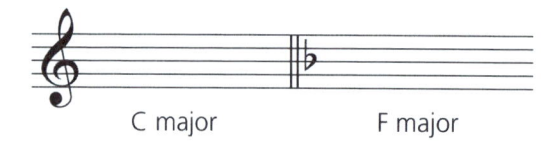

C major   F major

If the music is in a **minor key**, it will be in the **relative minor** of the major key for that key signature. A relative minor is always three semitones lower than its relative major.

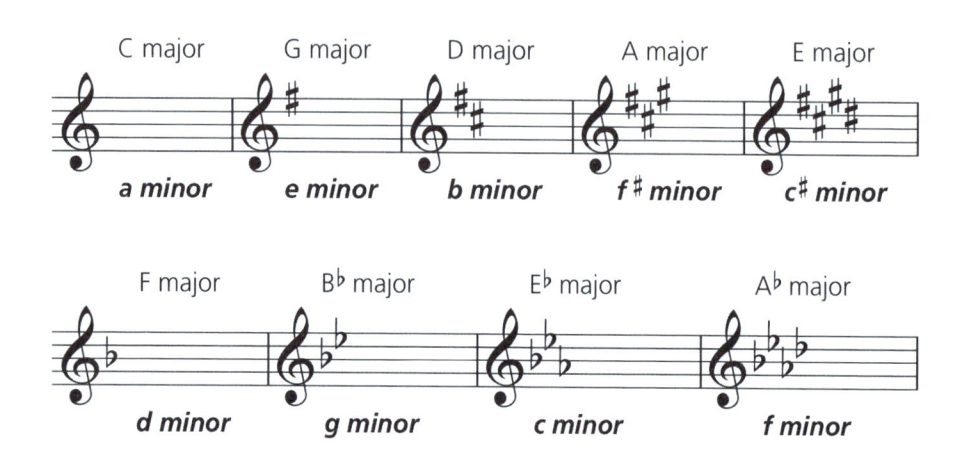

| C major | G major | D major | A major | E major |
| a minor | e minor | b minor | f♯ minor | c♯ minor |

| F major | B♭ major | E♭ major | A♭ major |
| d minor | g minor | c minor | f minor |

Melody

A melody is a series of notes, one after another. Melodies are often described as being made up of phrases.

A **phrase** is a group of notes that make sense together and express a distinct idea, but it takes more than one phrase to make a complete melody.

Words that describe the shape of a melody:

- repeated notes.
- stepwise motion (scale).
- interval leaps or jumps.
- ascending (upwards).
- descending (downwards).
- triadic.
- arpeggio (broken chord).
- countermelody.
- descant.

Score reading

At first, following the music of your set works (score reading) can be difficult. The first time you follow a score on your own:

- **Follow the score with your fingertips** or top of a pencil and tap the main beat (pulse) with your foot.
- Match what you hear with what you see.
- Check through the score marking for musical terms and symbols, and abbreviations for the instruments.
- Be aware of repeat signs and symbols (D.C. al fine, Dal Segno).
- Check the time signature/s and tempo marking and tempo changes for each section of music.
- Always listen out for easily recognisable instruments at certain points of the score. These pointers will help you if you get lost.

> **key point**
>
> **Dal Segno** means repeat the song from this symbol: 𝄋

5 Set Songs – Question 1

aims
- To develop a detailed appreciation of your set songs.
- To be familiar with the relevant musical terminology for the examination.

Question 1 is worth **30 marks**.
- Group A set songs will be examined in 2018.
- Group B set songs will be examined in 2016.
- Group C set songs will be examined in 2017.

exam focus

It is vital to be able to recognise all of your set songs. Listen to them many times, until you are thoroughly familiar with each song and its musical characteristics. You might hear a different version in the exam to what you hear in class, so be prepared.

exam TIPS

You **must** know:
- **The name of each song.**
- **The category from which each song comes.**
- **The composer of each song (if appropriate).**
- **Each song's musical features, such as:**

  1. Time signature.
  2. Key signature and tonality.
  3. Tempo.
  4. Country of origin.
  5. Type of song.
  6. Mood.
  7. Range of notes.
  8. Other musical features particular to each song. For example: syncopation, triplets, flattened seventh, ornamentation, musical sequences, specific melodic leaps.

What to expect in Question 1, Higher level

You will typically hear **three different song excerpts** from your eight set songs. Each excerpt should be played TWICE. There are usually four parts to Question 1: A, B, C, D.

Parts A, B and C are usually linked to the listening excerpts and are worth **8 marks each**. (There are at least two parts to each question: 4 marks + 4 marks.)

Part D (worth **6 marks**) usually consists of four bars of musical notation from one of the set songs that you have already heard in this question. You have to be able to identify which song the excerpt is from. You should be able to attempt to sightsing the given bars in your head. If you can't do this, quietly tap out the rhythm of the notation a number of times: this should help you decide which song excerpt it is.

Group A set songs

Category	Name of song
Irish folk songs	'An Mhaighdean Mhara'
Folk songs from other countries	'Kalinka'
Art songs	'The Little Sandman'
Historical and modern ballads	'Streets of Laredo'
Popular songs, spirituals, jazz songs	'The 59th Street Bridge Song' ('Feelin' Groovy')
Church music and carols	'The Wexford Carol'
Songs from operas, musicals, cantatas, oratorios	'Spring'
Two-part songs, rounds and canons	'Summer is icumen in'

1. Irish folk songs: 'An Mhaighdean Mhara'

Type of song	Lament from Northern Ireland
Date	Probably 18th century
Tonality	Major
Time signature	3/4
Tempo	Slow
Form	A B C D
Range	10th
Mood	Sad, solemn

exam focus

Songs recently examined:
- 'Sumer is icumen in' (2009).
- 'The Wexford Carol' (2009, 2006).
- 'The Little Sandman' (2009, 2003).
- 'Feelin' Groovy' (2006).
- 'Kalinka' (2006).

Melodic Features
- Ornamentation.
- Step movement.

Rhythmic Features
- Syncopation (e.g. quaver followed by dotted crotchet).
- Anacrusis (upbeat).

2. Folk songs from other countries: 'Kalinka'

Type of song	Russian wedding song
Date	1860
Tonality	Lah mode
Time signature	2/4
Tempo	Free tempo (rubato) and allegretto
Form	Chorus: A A1 A A1 Verse: B C B C1
Range	9th
Mood	Joyous

key point

'**Kalinka**' contains tempo changes: there are tempo changes in the chorus; and the verse is slower than the chorus.

Melodic Features
- Step movement.
- Repetition of phrases.

Rhythmic Features
- Anacrusis (upbeat).

3. Art songs: 'The Little Sandman'

Type of song	German Lied
Date	1858
Tonality	G major
Time signature	4/4
Tempo	Andante (walking pace)
Form	A A B C B C
Range	9th
Mood	Calm, serene
Composer	Brahms

Melodic Features
- Step movement.
- Leaps of 3rds and 4ths.

Rhythmic Features
- Anacrusis.
- Dotted crotchet/quaver motion.
- Simple rhythm.

4. Historical and modern ballads: 'Streets of Laredo'

Type of song	Historical ballad from the US
Date	19th century
Tonality	F major
Time signature	3/4
Tempo	Moderate
Form	A B A B1
Range	Octave
Mood	Contented

Melodic Features
- Step movement.
- Repeated notes.

Rhythmic Features
- Anacrusis.
- Dotted crotchet/quaver motion.

5. Popular songs, spirituals, jazz songs: 'The 59th Street Bridge Song (Feelin' Groovy)'

Type of song	Popular song from the US
Date	1966
Tonality	B flat major
Time signature	C (common time)
Tempo	Moderately fast
Form	3 verses (varied melody in each one)
Range	10th
Mood	Joyful
Composer	Paul Simon

Melodic Features
- Change of melody in verse 3.
- Intervals of 3rds.

Rhythmic Features
- Syncopation.
- Triplets.
- Rests at beginning of phrases.
- Tied notes.

6. Church music and carols: 'The Wexford Carol'

Type of song	Irish Christmas Carol
Date	17th/18th century
Tonality	G major
Time signature	3/4
Tempo	Slowly
Form	A A1 B A1 (Ternary)
Range	10th
Mood	Cheerful, devout

Melodic Features
- Flattened 3rd.
- Repeated final note.
- Flattened 7th.
- Leap of a 7th.

Rhythmic Features
- Syncopation.
- Fermata (pause) on final note.
- Anacrusis.

7. Songs from operas, musicals, cantatas, oratorios: 'Spring'

Type of song	Aria from Germany
Date	1723, from the opera *Ottone*
Tonality	E major
Time signature	4/4
Tempo	Andante
Form	A B A (Da Capo Aria form)
Range	10th
Mood	Joyful
Composer	Handel

Melodic Features
- Ornamentation.
- Modulation to C# minor in B section.
- Melismatic word setting.
- Sequence.
- Word painting.

Rhythmic Features
- Dotted rhythm.
- Fermata (pause).
- Use of quaver/semiquaver figure.

8. Two-part songs, rounds and canons: 'Sumer is icumen in'

Type of song	Six-part canon/double round from England
Date	13th/14th century
Tonality	Major
Time signature	6/8
Tempo	Allegretto
Form	Double round
Range	9th
Mood	Happy
Composer	John of Fornsete

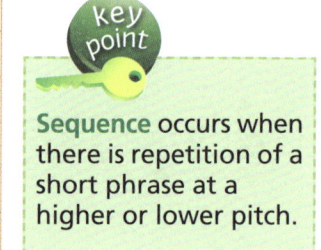

> **key point**
> **Sequence** occurs when there is repetition of a short phrase at a higher or lower pitch.

Melodic Features
- Step movement.
- Leaps of a 3rd.
- Polyphonic texture.

Rhythmic Features
- Dance rhythm.
- 6/8 compound time.

SET SONGS – QUESTION 1

HIGHER LEVEL QUESTION 1, 2009

Question 1: Set Songs (30 marks)
THREE excerpts, each played TWICE.
Answer A, B, C and D.

Note: Musical excerpts from past exam papers are available at www.examinations.ie

A Excerpt 1

(i) This is an example of
- an aria
- a song with descant
- a round
- a duet

(ii) Give a reason for your answer.

(8)

B Excerpt 2

(i) Name this song.

(ii) On which words do we hear a flattened seventh?
- Near Bethlehem ☐
- Flocks of lambs ☐
- Shepherds keep ☐
- Feeding sheep ☐

(8)

C Excerpt 3

(i) The composer of this song is:

(ii) A rhythmic feature is:

(8)

D

Here is an excerpt from one of the songs you have just heard.

It is the opening of:
- song 1 ☐
- song 2 ☐
- song 3 ☐

(6)

ORDINARY LEVEL QUESTION 1, 2009

Question 1: Set Songs (30 marks)
THREE excerpts, each played TWICE.
Answer A, B and C.

A Excerpt 1
(i) This song is an example of:
- a lullaby
- a waltz
- a round

(ii) It welcomes:
- spring
- summer
- autumn

(10)

B Excerpt 2
(i) Name this song:

(ii) The form of this song is:
- A A B A
- A B C A
- A A B B

(10)

C Excerpt 3
(i) The name of this song is:
- The Little Sandman
- Spring
- Kalinka

(ii) The composer is:
- Mozart
- Brahms
- Schubert

(10)

Group B set songs

Category	Name of Song
Irish folk songs	'Amhrán na Cuiginne'
Folk songs from other countries	'Click go the Shears'
Art songs	'Wanderer's Night Song'
Historical and modern ballads	'The Verdant Braes of Screen'
Popular songs, spirituals, jazz songs	'Yesterday'
Church music and carols	'The Lord is my Shepherd'
Songs from operas, musicals, cantatas, oratorios	'Can't Help Lovin' Dat Man'
Two-part songs, rounds and canons	'Evening Prayer'

1. Irish folk songs: 'Amhrán na Cuiginne'

Type of song	Working song and love song from Ireland
Date	Probably 18th century
Tonality	Major
Time signature	6/8
Tempo	Lively
Form	Verse and chorus
Range	Octave
Mood	Gentle

Melodic Features
- Step movement.
- Repeated final note.
- Flattened 7th.

Rhythmic Features
- Simple rhythm.
- 6/8 compound time.

Songs recently examined:
- 'Can't Help Lovin' Dat Man' (2010, 2004).
- 'Wanderer's Night Song' (2010).
- 'Yesterday' (2010, 2007).
- 'Click go the Shears' (2007, 2004).
- 'The Verdant Braes of Screen' (2007).

2. Folk songs from other countries: 'Click go the Shears'

Type of song	Australian working song
Date	19th century
Tonality	Major
Time signature	4/4
Tempo	Lively
Form	Verse: A B A C Chorus: D E A C
Range	10th
Mood	Lively

Melodic Features
- Step movement.
- Descending scales.
- Repeated final note.
- Descending scales.
- Octave leaps.

Rhythmic Features
- Dotted rhythms.

3. Art songs: 'Wanderer's Night Song'

Type of song	Lied, written in Austria
Date	1823
Tonality	Major
Time signature	C (common time)
Tempo	Slowly
Form	Through-composed
Range	Octave
Mood	Peaceful
Composer	Schubert

key point

A **lied** is a romantic German poem set to music.

Melodic Features
- Flattened 3rd.
- Sequence.
- Repeated notes.

Rhythmic Features
- Dotted rhythms.
- Fermata (pause).

4. Historical and modern ballads: 'The Verdant Braes of Screen'

Type of song	English language ballad from Co. Derry
Date	19th century
Tonality	Major
Time signature	4/4
Tempo	Fairly slow
Form	Through-composed
Range	Octave
Mood	Subdued

Melodic Features
- Flattened 7th.

Rhythmic Features
- Triplet.
- Syncopation.
- Anacrusis.

5. Popular songs, spirituals, jazz songs: 'Yesterday'

Type of song	English pop song
Date	1965
Tonality	Major
Time signature	2/2 (split common time)
Tempo	Moderate
Form	Ternary A A B A
Range	10th
Mood	Sad and regretful
Composer	John Lennon and Paul McCartney

Melodic Features
- Step movement.
- Ascending and descending scales.
- Repeated notes.

Rhythmic Features
- Syncopation.
- Pause on final note.

6. Church music and carols: 'The Lord is my Shepherd'

Type of song	Setting of Psalm 23
Date	1970
Tonality	Lah mode
Time signature	3/4 in refrain; free time in verse
Tempo	Slow; free tempo in verse
Form	Refrain and verse
Range	Octave
Mood	Reverent
Composer	Arranged by Fr Tom Egan

Melodic Features
- Ornamentation (triplet in refrain).
- Repeated notes.

Rhythmic Features
- Triplet rhythm.
- Anacrusis.
- Free rhythm in verses.

key point

The verses in this song are written in **plainchant**. Features of this style include:
- Syllabic (one note per syllable) or melismatic (many notes per syllable).
- Sung in Latin.
- Free rhythm.
- No bar lines.
- Unaccompanied.

7. Songs from operas, musicals, cantatas, oratorios: 'Can't Help Lovin' Dat Man'

Type of song	Solo song from the musical *Showboat*
Date	1927
Tonality	Major
Time signature	2/2 (Split common time)
Tempo	Moderate
Form	Ternary: A A B A
Range	11th
Mood	Joyful
Composer	Jerome Kern

SET SONGS – QUESTION 1

Melodic Features
- Flattened 3rds and 6ths.
- Triadic melody.
- Sequence.

Rhythmic Features
- Syncopation.

8. Two-part songs, rounds and canons: 'Evening Prayer'

Type of song	Duet from the German opera *Hänsel und Gretel*
Date	1893
Tonality	Major
Time signature	4/4
Tempo	Moderate
Form	Through-composed
Range	11th
Mood	Quiet and calm
Composer	Engelbert Humperdinck

key point

The texture of this song is **homophonic** and **polyphonic**. The opening 8 bars are homophonic and the voices imitate each other for the remainder of the verse (polyphonic).

Melodic Features
- Rising sequences.
- Key changes.
- Opening bar based on doh triad.

Rhythmic Features
- Crotchet movement.
- *Poco rit.* means 'a little slower'.
- *A tempo* means back to the original speed.

HIGHER LEVEL QUESTION 1, 2010

Question 1: Set Songs (30 marks)
THREE excerpts, each played TWICE.
Answer A, B, C and D.

A Excerpt 1
(i) Name the stage musical from which this song is taken.
_____

(ii) Name **one** jazz feature that you hear in the excerpt.
_____
(8)

B Excerpt 2
(i) This song was composed by:
_____

(ii) It is a **lied**. Give **two** features of a lied.

1 _____
2 _____
(8)

C Excerpt 3
(i) Using letters, give the form of this song.
_____

(ii) This form is:
- binary ☐
- ternary ☐
- rondo ☐
- free ☐

_____
(8)

D
Here is an excerpt from one of the songs you have just heard.

It is the opening of:
- song 1 ☐
- song 2 ☐
- song 3 ☐

_____
(6)

ORDINARY LEVEL QUESTION 1, 2010

Question 1: Set Songs (30 marks)
THREE excerpts, each played TWICE.
Answer A, B and C.

A Excerpt 1

This song is taken from:
- Cats ☐
- Showboat ☐
- Oklahoma! ☐

The song begins with:
- 3 repeated notes ☐
- 4 repeated notes ☐
- 5 repeated notes ☐

(10)

B Excerpt 2

This is:
- an art song ☐
- a religious song ☐
- a ballad ☐

The composer is:
- Humperdinck ☐
- Kern ☐
- Schubert ☐

(10)

C Excerpt 3

This song was written in:
- 1955 ☐
- 1965 ☐
- 1975 ☐

The form is:
- A A B A ☐
- A A B B ☐
- A A B C ☐

(10)

Group C set songs

Category	Name of Song
Irish folk songs	'Preab san Ól'
Folk songs from other countries	'Muss i Denn'
Art songs	'Caro Mio Ben' ('Come Happy Spring')
Historical and modern ballads	'Streets of London'
Popular songs, spirituals, jazz songs	'This Little Light of Mine'
Church music and carols	'Salve Regina'
Songs from operas, musicals, cantatas, oratorios	'Oh, I Got Plenty of Nuttin''
Two-part songs, rounds and canons	'By the Waters of Babylon'

1. Irish folk songs: 'Preab san Ól'

Type of song	Drinking song from Ireland
Date	Probably 18th century
Tonality	Major
Time signature	3/4
Tempo	Lively
Form	Ternary A A B A
Range	9th
Mood	Lively

exam focus

Songs recently examined:
- 'By the Waters of Babylon' (2008).
- 'Muss i Denn' (2008).
- 'Caro Mio Ben' (2008).
- 'This Little Light of Mine' (2005).
- 'Preab san Ól' (2005).
- 'Oh, I Got Plenty of Nuttin'' (2005).

Melodic Features
- Repeated notes.
- Repetition of phrases.
- Steps and leaps.

Rhythmic Features
- Anacrusis.
- Simple rhythm patterns.

SET SONGS – QUESTION 1   41

2. Folk songs from other countries: 'Muss i Denn'

Type of song	Love song from Germany
Date	Unknown
Tonality	Major
Time signature	4/4
Tempo	Moderate
Form	Ternary A A B A1
Range	Octave
Mood	Happy

Interesting fact!
The melody of this song was used by Elvis Presley in a pop version called 'Wooden Heart'.

Melodic Features
- Sequences.
- Use of 3rds.
- Step movement.

Rhythmic Features
- Anacrusis.
- Simple rhythm patterns.

3. Art songs: 'Caro Mio Ben' (Come Happy Spring)

Type of song	Italian Aria
Date	1780s
Tonality	Major
Time signature	C (common time)
Tempo	Quite slow
Form	Ternary A A1 B A2
Range	10th
Mood	Calm
Composer	Giordani

Melodic Features
- Sequences.
- Ornamentation.
- Descending phrases.

Rhythmic Features
- Dotted rhythms.
- Begins on 3rd beat of bar.
- Fermata (pause).

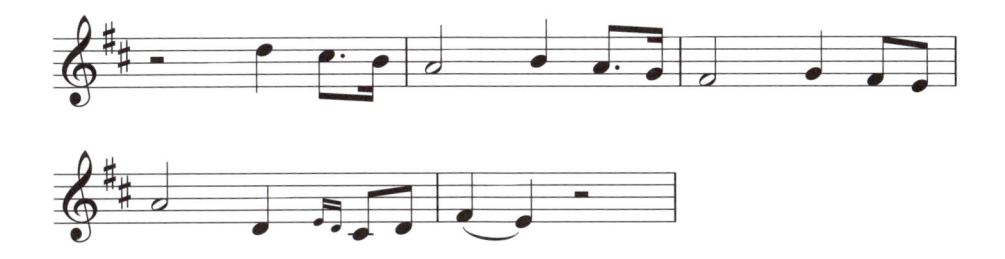

4. Historical and modern ballads: 'Streets of London'

Type of song	Protest ballad from England
Date	1969
Tonality	Major
Time signature	Split common time
Tempo	Moderate
Form	Ternary: A A1 B A1
Range	Octave
Mood	Sad
Composer	Ralph McTell

Melodic Features
- Repeated notes.
- Triadic melody.

Rhythmic Features
- Syncopation.

5. Popular songs, spirituals, jazz songs: 'This Little Light of Mine'

Type of song	Christian spiritual from the US
Date	Unknown
Tonality	Major
Time signature	4/4
Tempo	Lively
Form	Ternary A B A (Chorus, verse, chorus)
Range	6th
Mood	Joyful
Composer	Words from the Gospel of St Matthew

Melodic Features
- Flattened 3rd (blues note).
- Repeated notes.
- Repetition of phrases.

Rhythmic Features
- Syncopation.
- Anacrusis in the verse.

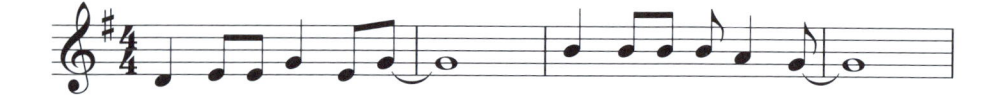

SET SONGS – QUESTION 1   43

6. Church music and carols: 'Salve Regina'

Type of song	Plainchant from Europe
Date	Maybe early 13th century
Tonality	Modal
Time signature	Free time
Tempo	Free tempo
Form	Through-composed
Range	6th
Mood	Spiritual

Melodic Features
- Mostly syllabic word setting.
- Melismas in final phrases.

Rhythmic Features
- Free rhythm.
- No time signature.
- No bar lines.

exam focus

This song is written in **plainchant**. Make sure you can discuss the features of plainchant!

key point

The texture of this song is **monophonic**. This is where there is one single line of melody without accompaniment.

7. Songs from operas, musicals, cantatas, oratorios: 'Oh, I Got Plenty of Nuttin''

Type of song	From the opera *Porgy and Bess*
Date	1935, US
Tonality	Major
Time signature	4/4
Tempo	Moderate
Form	Ternary A A1 B A Coda
Range	10th
Mood	Joyful
Composer	Gershwin

Melodic Features
- Rising sequences.
- Sharpened 4ths.
- Unusual E# accidental.
- Repeated notes.

Rhythmic Features
- Syncopation.
- Spoken triplets.
- Anacrusis.

8. Two-part songs, rounds and canons: 'By the Waters of Babylon'

Type of song	3-part round, based on Psalm 136
Date	Unknown
Tonality	Minor
Time signature	4/4
Tempo	Slow
Form	A B C
Range	10th
Mood	Distressing, sad

Melodic Features
- Falling sequences.
- Repeated notes.

Rhythmic Features
- Short, rhythmic ideas in each phrase.

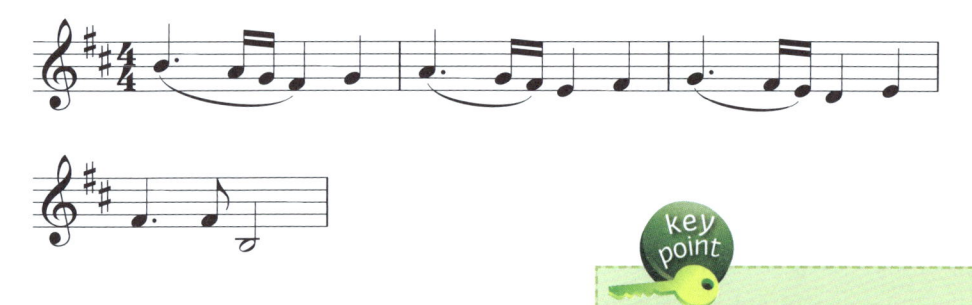

key point

The texture of this song is **polyphonic**. It is sung as a three-part round where the voices **imitate** each other.

SET SONGS – QUESTION 1   45

HIGHER LEVEL QUESTION 1, 2008

Question 1: Set Songs (30 marks)
THREE excerpts, each played TWICE.
Answer A, B, C and D.

A Excerpt 1
(i) This is an example of:
- an aria ☐
- a round ☐
- an art song ☐
- a spiritual ☐

(ii) What melodic feature is heard in each of the three phrases?
_____
(8)

B Excerpt 2
(i) The form of this song is:
- A B C A ☐
- A A B A ☐
- A A B B ☐
- A B B A ☐

(ii) Who made this song famous?
- Ralph McTell ☐
- George Gershwin ☐
- Elvis Presley ☐
- Shaun Davey ☐

(8)

C Excerpt 3
(i) The *melody* begins on the:
- 1st beat ☐
- 2nd beat ☐
- 3rd beat ☐
- 4th beat ☐

(ii) This song contains examples of:
- free rhythm ☐
- triplets ☐
- dotted rhythm ☐
- syncopation ☐

(8)

D Here is an excerpt from one of the songs you have just heard.

It is the opening of:
- song 1 ☐
- song 2 ☐
- song 3 ☐

(6)

ORDINARY LEVEL QUESTION 1, 2008

Question 1: Set Songs (30 marks)
THREE excerpts, each played TWICE.
Answer A, B, C and D.

A Excerpt 1
(i) The name of the city in the title of this song is:
- London ☐
- Dublin ☐
- Babylon ☐

(ii) This song is an example of:
- an aria ☐
- a round ☐
- an art song ☐

(10)

B Excerpt 2
This song comes from:
- Scotland ☐
- Germany ☐
- America ☐

The form is:
- A A B A ☐
- A A B B ☐
- A A B C ☐

(10)

C Excerpt 3
(i) Name this song: _____

(ii) The composer is:
- Handel ☐
- Giordani ☐
- Humperdinck ☐

(10)

6 Set Works – Question 2

aims
- To be able to approach your set works question with confidence.
- To be familiar with the instrumental sounds and main features of your set works.

exam focus

It is vital to be able to recognise the sounds of the different instruments, especially those playing a solo melody. To prepare well for the exam you should listen to your set works many times. This will help you become more familiar with the different melodies and instrumental sounds.

Question 2 is worth **30 marks**.

- Group A set works will be examined in 2018.
- Group B set works will be examined in 2016.
- Group C set works will be examined in 2017.

Each group contains *three* different set works. Some of the set works are longer than others and some have more than one movement that you must study. Each year the set works from Group A, B and C alternate.

You **MUST** know:

- The title of the whole work, the name of each work on your course and the section of each work on your course.
- The name of the composer and some background details about their style of composition and historical period (e.g. Baroque, Romantic, etc.).
- All score-reading directions, performance directions and musical terminology used in the scores, including all instruments that are used in each work or section of the work.
- All the general musical features, instrumental and compositional techniques for each work, such as:
    1. Time signature.
    2. Key signature and tonality.
    3. Tempo.
    4. Genre of work.
    5. Instrumental medium.
    6. Other musical features particular to each work.

You must be able to recognise all your set works by ear. Remember that the listening excerpt could be very different from what you hear in class or what is on your CD of set works: a different version may be played in the Question 2 excerpt.

> **key point**
> Revise Chapter 4 so that you are familiar with musical styles.

What to expect in Question 2

You will typically hear **one or two excerpts from ONE of your set works**. The first excerpt should be played THREE times, the second, if there is one, will be played TWICE. There are usually several parts to Question 2: short questions; longer discussion; and compare or explain questions.

The first questions are usually linked to the listening excerpt, of which there is a **printed score**. These questions are usually about recognising:

- The title of the work or section of the work.
- The composer.
- The instruments playing the excerpt.
- Musical features you can hear or see on the printed score.

If there is a second excerpt from the set work, you may be asked to:

- 'State and explain new musical features in this excerpt' (2006 paper).
- Compare or contrast changes in the music or instrumentation from the first excerpt.
- Explain musical terms from this section of the work.

This question is largely based on aural recognition, but it really helps to have a solid knowledge of all your set works. Listen to your set works and set songs CDs frequently in your own time, until you are thoroughly familiar with each work.

Musical terminology and symbols used in set works

8va – play an octave higher than written.
A tempo – back to the original speed.
Affetuoso – slowly and tenderly.
Alla marcia e molto marcato – like a march and much accented.
Allargando – broadly.

Pesante – peasant-like, very heavy and exaggerated.
Picc., Fl., Ob. – piccolo, flute and oboe.
Più – more.
Piu Vivo – more lively.
Poco – little.

SET WORKS – QUESTION 2

Allegretto moderato – moderately fast.
Allegretto pastorale – moderately fast in a pastoral style.
Allegro deciso – steady fast tempo.
Allegro vivace – fast and lively.
Allegro – fast.
Andante – at a walking pace.
Andante moderato ma con moto – at a walking pace, but with movement.
Andantino – slowly.
Arco – play with the bow.
Bsn. – bassoon.
Cantabile – sweetly, in a song-like manner.
Cls. – clarinets.
Con sordini – play with mutes.
Cor. Ang. – cor anglais.
Cresc. – crescendo, getting louder.
D.C. al Fine – go back to the start and play until the word Fine.
DBs – double basses.
Fine – the end (after the final repeat).
Hns. – horns.
Legato – play smoothly.
Molto dim. – becoming a lot softer.
Molto – much.

Poco string(endo) – building and speeding up a little.
Rinforz(ando) – extremely loud.
Rubato – stolen time: slightly slowing down the tempo of the piece.
Sax. – saxophone.
sf – suddenly loud.
Solo Vcs – solo cellos.
Sotto voce – with a hushed quality.
Stretto poco a poco – pushing, little by little.
Stringendo – building to a climax, accelerating.
Strs. – strings.
Tbn. – trombone.
Tempo di mazurka – at the speed of a mazurka (fairly fast).
Timp. – timpani.
Tpts. – trumpets.
tr. – a trill.
Tr. – triangle.
Tr. ~~~~ – drum roll on timpani (trill).
Tranquillo – tranquil.
Tutti – full orchestra playing.
Vla. – viola.
Vlns. + Obs. – violins and oboes.
WW – woodwind.

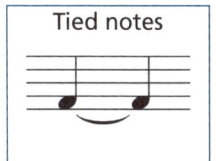

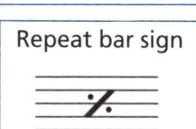

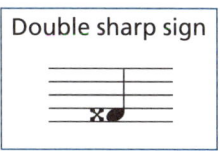

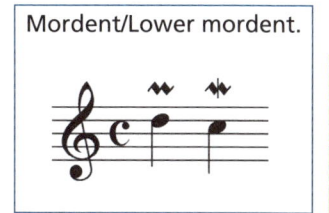

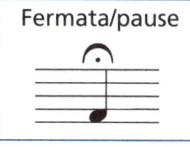

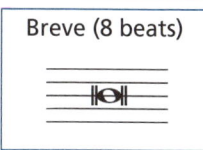

Tied notes	Staccato sign	Grace note	Tremolo
Repeat bar sign	Double sharp sign	Fermata/pause	Breve (8 beats)
Tenuto (held)			
Marcato – a marked accent	Mordent/Lower mordent.		

> **key point**
>
> A **mordent** sign instructs the player to quickly play the written note, then the note *higher*, then return rapidly to the written note.
>
> A **lower mordent** sign instructs the player to quickly play the written note, then the note *lower*, then return rapidly to the written note.

Group A set works

Work	Section(s)	Composer	Date
Water Music (Suite in D major)	Hornpipe Minuet	George Frideric Handel	1717
Overture to *William Tell*	Sunrise in the Alps Storm Shepherd on the Mountainside Revolution	Gioachino Rossini	1829
Carmina Burana	O Fortuna	Carl Orff	1937

exam focus

Works recently examined:
- Water Music (Minuet) (2009).
- *William Tell* (Shepherd on the Mountainside) (2006).
- Water Music (Hornpipe) (2003).

Handel's Water Music

- This work was a commission for King George I, for a party he was having on the River Thames in London in 1717.
- The Water Music consists of 17 **movements** which are divided into 3 **suites**.
- It is composed in the **Baroque** style.

key point
A **suite** is a collection of dances.
A **movement** is a section of music.

Hornpipe

A **hornpipe** is a popular English dance with three beats in a bar.

The instruments used in this section of Handel's Water Music are as follows:

Strings	Woodwind	Brass
Violin, viola, cello, double bass.	Oboe, bassoon.	Trumpet, horn.

SET WORKS – QUESTION 2

Time signature	3/2 (three minim beats per bar)
Key signature/tonality	D major
Form	A B A (Ternary)
Mood	Joyful
Tempo	Lively

Musical features (Section A)

- Opening theme contains **syncopated** rhythm.
- Use of **trills**.
- Repeated notes.
- Melody played in **3rds**.
- **Key change** to A major.
- Repetition of phrases.
- Answering between the instrumental groups.
- **Perfect cadence** in D major at end of section.

Musical features (Section B)

- Contrasting section in **B minor**.
- **Quieter** with no horns or trumpets.
- More **quaver** movement.
- Repeated notes.
- **Syncopation**.
- **Perfect cadence** in B minor at end of section.

Note that **Section A is repeated** in the piece.

The **texture** of this section is mainly **homophonic** – the main tune is supported by chordal accompaniment.

HIGHER LEVEL QUESTION 2, 2003

Question 2: Set Works (30 marks)
An excerpt from one of your set works will be played THREE times.
An outline of the music score is printed below.
Answer A, B, C and D (sample answers are included).

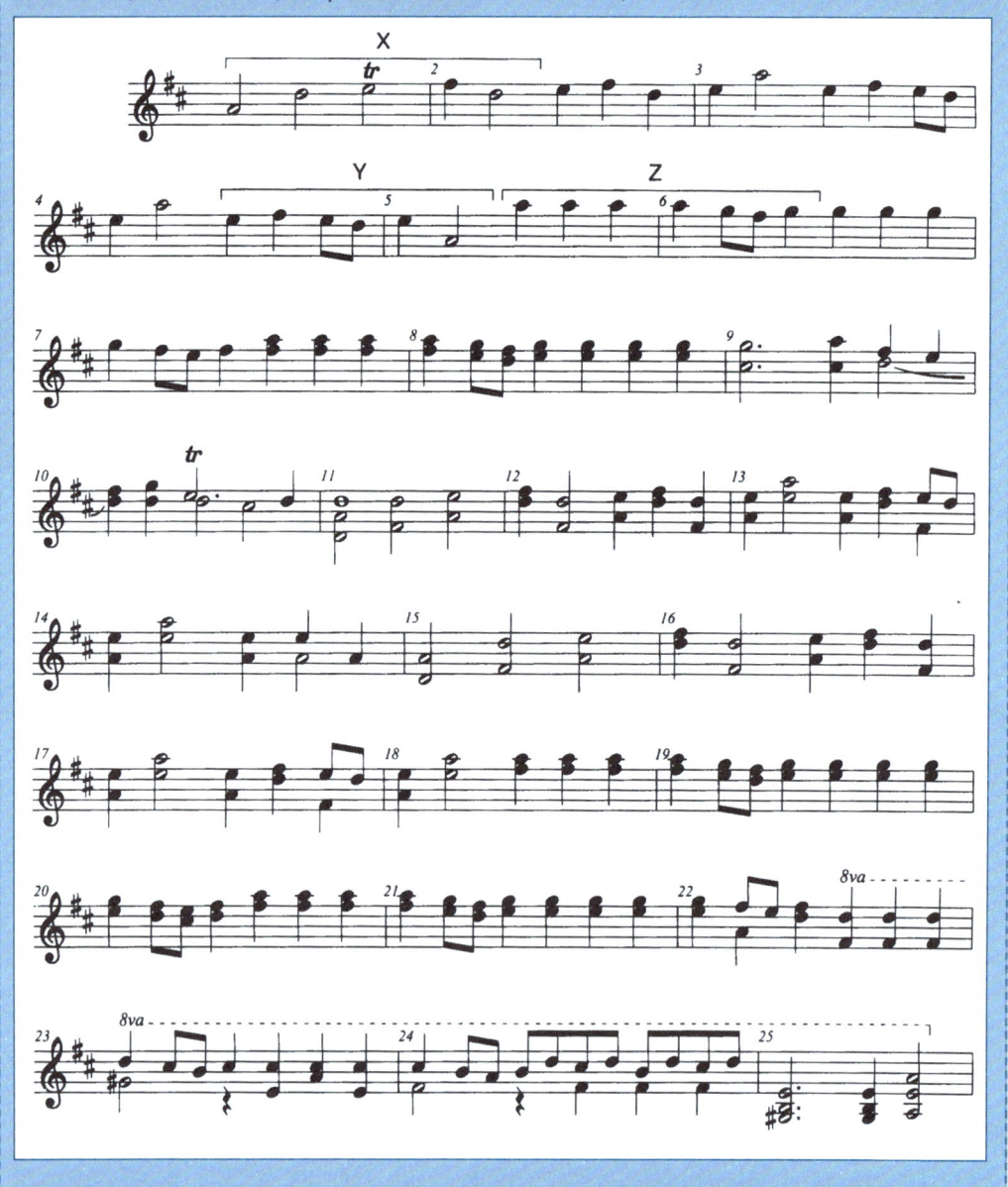

A Who composed this music?

G.F. Handel

SET WORKS – QUESTION 2   53

Why did he write it?
Handel was commissioned to write a piece of music for King George I, who was having a barge party on the River Thames.

(5)

B This is a dance. Give the title.
Hornpipe

The time signature is
- 3/4   • 3/2   • 2/2
3/2

(5)

C Which family of instruments does NOT feature in this excerpt?
• brass   • strings   • percussion   • woodwind
Percussion

Name the family of instruments on bars 1–10.
Strings

(6)

D Which solo instrument plays the melody in bars 11–14?
Trumpet

Which solo instrument plays the melody in bars 15–18?
French horn

(6)

Now listen to a later section which is not printed here. You will hear it TWICE. Answer E.

E This section begins with a musical idea already heard in the first excerpt. It is based on one of the following in the music score above.
• X   • Y   • Z
Z

List TWO features of the music that follows.
1 *Minor key*
2 *No trumpets or horns*

(8)

Minuet

A **minuet** is a dance form of French origin with three beats in a bar.

Time signature	3/4
Key signature/tonality	B minor
Form	A B (Binary)
Mood	Joyful
Tempo	Moderate

Musical features (Section A)

- Repeated notes.
- Sequence.
- Simple melody that is repeated.
- Trills.
- Mainly step movement.

Musical features (Section B)

- New tune, 8 bars longer.
- Repeated notes.
- More quaver movement.
- This section is also repeated.

The **texture** of this section is **homophonic**.

SET WORKS – QUESTION 2

HIGHER LEVEL QUESTION 2, 2009

Question 2: Set Works (30 marks)
An excerpt from one of your set works will be played THREE times.
The melody, up to bar 8, is printed below.
Answer A, B, C and D.

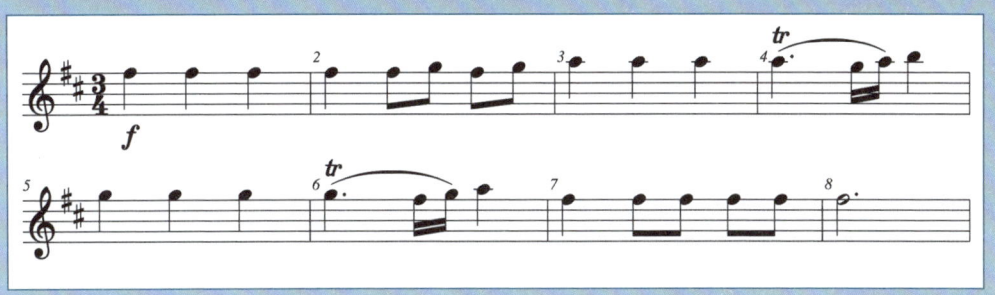

A

(i) This piece was composed in:

- 1617
- 1717
- 1817
- 1917

(ii) Briefly state why it was written.

(5)

B

(i) This is:

- a gigue
- a hornpipe
- a minuet
- a gavotte

(ii) It is part of a suite. Explain the term suite.

(5)

C

(i) The range of the melody in bars 1–8 is:

- a fourth
- a fifth
- a sixth
- an octave

(ii) The instruments in this section include:

- horns and trumpets
- violins and trumpets
- oboes and horns
- strings only

(4)

D

(i) The form of the whole excerpt is:
- A A B A
- A A B B
- A B B A
- A B A B

_____

(ii) This is called _____ form.

(4)

Now listen to another excerpt from the same work, which is not printed here.
It will be played TWICE.
Answer E.

E Comment on this excerpt under each of the headings below.

(i) Type of dance:
_____

(ii) Time signature:
_____

(iii) Key:
_____

(iv) One melodic feature:
_____

(12)

Rossini's Overture to *William Tell*

- This is the complete Overture to Rossini's last opera, *William Tell*, which was composed in 1829.
- The Overture is an example of **programme music**, which describes a scene or tells a story. In this case it is the legend of the Swiss hero William Tell.
- This is composed in the **Romantic** style.

The instruments used in the work are as follows:

Strings	Woodwind	Brass	Percussion
Violin, viola, cello, double bass.	Flute, oboe, clarinet, bassoon, piccolo, cor anglais.	Trumpet, trombone, horn.	Timpani, triangle, cymbals, bass drum.

Section A – Sunrise in the Alps

Time signature	3/4
Key signature/tonality	E minor, changes to E major
Mood	Peaceful
Tempo	Andante (fairly slow)

Musical features

- 5 solo **cellos**.
- Rising E minor **arpeggio**.
- Trills.
- Grace notes.
- Triplets.
- Staccato notes.
- Key change to **E major**.
- **Homophonic** texture.

Section B – Storm

Time signature	4/4
Key signature/tonality	G major
Mood	Dramatic
Tempo	Allegro (Fast)

Musical features

- Contrasting **dynamics** (*pp*, *ff*).
- Ascending and descending **chromatic scales**.
- **Trombones** are prominent in this section.
- Semiquaver movement on strings (rustling of the wind).
- **Staccato** woodwind notes (raindrops).
- **Homophonic** and **polyphonic** textures.

Section C – Shepherd on the Mountainside

Time signature	3/8
Key signature/tonality	G major
Mood	Calm and peaceful
Tempo	Andantino (a little faster than Andante)

Musical features

- Main tune is played on the **cor anglais**.
- **Homophonic** texture.
- Main tune repeated on **flute**.
- **Pizzicato** strings accompany.
- Triangle introduced on first beat of each bar (cow bell).
- **Descant** on flute above cor anglais melody produces a **polyphonic** texture.
- **Triplet** rhythm.

Section D – Revolution

Time signature	2/4
Key signature/tonality	E major
Mood	Lively, exciting
Tempo	Allegro vivace (fast and lively)

Musical features

- **Brass fanfare** based on doh triad.
- **Contrasting dynamics**.
- Repeated notes.
- **Staccato** notes.
- **Syncopated** rhythms.
- Mostly semiquaver movement.
- **Homophonic** texture.

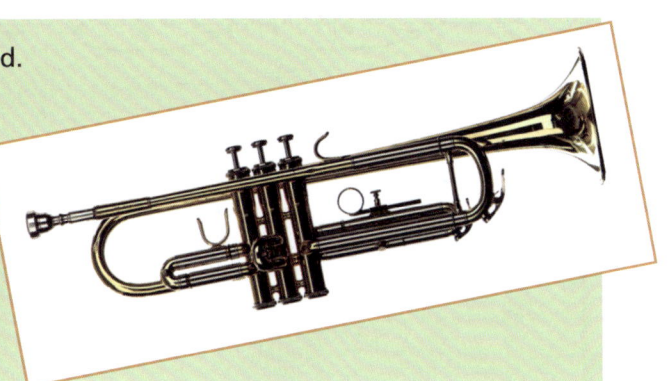

HIGHER LEVEL QUESTION 2, 2006

Question 2: Set Works (30 marks)
An excerpt from one of your set works will be played THREE times.
An outline of the music score is printed below.
Answer A, B, C and D. (Sample answers are included).

A

(i) This excerpt is called
- Sunrise in the Alps
- Storm
- Shepherd on a Mountainside
- Revolution

Shepherd on a Mountainside

(ii) State the type of work from which it is taken.
Overture

(6)

B

(i) What solo instrument plays in bars 1–5?
Cor anglais

(ii) The melody in bars 6–10 is different. Give <u>one</u> difference.
The melody is played on the flute.

(6)

C

(i) The time signature is
- $\frac{3}{4}$
- $\frac{3}{8}$
- $\frac{4}{4}$
- $\frac{6}{8}$

$\frac{3}{8}$

(ii) Give <u>one</u> bar where a trill is heard.
Bar 4

(4)

D

(i) Suggest a word or two to describe the mood.
Calm and gentle.

(ii) State how the composer creates this mood.
High-pitched instruments, soft dynamics, sustained pp chords.

(6)

Now listen to a later section, which is not printed here.
It will be played TWICE.
Answer E.

E

(i) State two new musical features in this excerpt.
  1 *Countermelody on flute*
  2 *Sequences*

(ii) Briefly explain <u>one</u> of them.
Countermelody on flute: the flute plays a new, high-pitched melody above the main tune.

(8)

Orff's *Carmina Burana* – O Fortuna (First movement)

- O Fortuna is the first movement from German composer Carl Orff's cantata *Carmina Burana*.
- A **cantata** is a musical composition, often using a religious text, for chorus and orchestra.
- O Fortuna is based on a simple three-note melodic motif.
- This is composed in the twentieth-century modern style.

The instruments used in this work are as follows:

Strings	Woodwind	Brass	Percussion	Voices
Violin, viola, cello, double bass.	Piccolo, flute, oboe, clarinet, cor anglais, bass clarinet, bassoon, double bassoon.	Trumpet, trombone, horn, tuba.	Timpani, glockenspiel, xylophone, castanet, bells, bass drum, gong, tambourine, piano.	Soprano, alto, tenor, bass.

Time signature	3/1 and 3/2
Key signature/tonality	D minor (lah mode)
Form	Unitary: A A1 A2
Mood	Exciting, joyful
Tempo	Slow intro, faster verses

Musical features (Intro)

- **Dramatic** chorus and orchestra.
- **Accented** notes.
- Dynamic is *ff*.
- **High** vocal range.
- Fermata (pause) on final note.

SET WORKS – QUESTION 2

Features of Verse 1 (A)

- Dynamic is *pp*.
- Speed is doubled.
- **Staccato** notes.
- Melody based on a **three-note pattern**.
- Chorus begins in **unison**, then in harmony of **3rds**.
- Use of **rests** and **syncopation**.

Features of Verse 2 (A1)

- Almost identical to Verse 1.
- **Clarinets** are added to the accompaniment.

Features of Verse 3 (A2)

- The music gets **suddenly loud**.
- **Full orchestra** plays the accompaniment.
- Melody is the same but sung an **octave higher** by sopranos.
- Harmony in **3rds** is added.
- **Speed increases** towards the end.
- The final note is held for 9 bars.
- The movement ends on a **D major chord**.
- The texture of this movement is **homophonic**.

Group B set works

Work	Section(s)	Composer	Date
Brandenburg Concerto No. 5 in D major	First Movement Second Movement	Johann Sebastian Bach	1721
Peer Gynt Suite No. 1	Morning Anitra's Dance In the Hall of the Mountain King	Edward Grieg	1874
Rodeo	Hoe-Down	Aaron Copland	1942

exam focus

Works recently examined:
- Peer Gynt Suite No. 1 (Morning) (2010).
- *Rodeo* (Hoe-Down) (2007).
- Brandenburg Concerto No. 5 (First movement) (2004).
- Peer Gynt Suite No. 1 (Anitra's Dance) (2001).

Bach's Brandenburg Concerto No. 5 in D major

- Bach wrote this concerto for the private orchestra of the Margrave of Brandenburg.
- It is composed in the Baroque style.
- **Ritornello form** means that the main musical theme returns several times during the movement.
- There is an **episode** (new material) in between the recurring main theme.
- **Continuo** is the word used to describe the continuous bass line played by the harpsichord and lower strings.

key point

A **concerto grosso** is a piece of music for a group of soloists **(concertino)** and an accompanying orchestra **(ripieno/tutti)**.

The instruments used in this work are as follows:

Concertino	Ripieno/Tutti	Continuo
Violin, flute, harpsichord.	Violin, viola, cello, double bass.	Harpsichord, cello, double bass.

First Movement – Allegro

Time signature	C (common time)
Key signature/tonality	D major
Form	Ritornello
Mood	Bright
Tempo	Fast and lively

Musical features

- Opening **ritornello** theme played in semiquavers, based on **rising arpeggio** and **descending scale**.
- The texture of the ritornello theme is **homophonic**.
- The **episodes** are played by the solo flute and solo violin in **imitation** supported by the harpsichord.
- The texture of the episodes is **polyphonic**.
- **Key changes** to A major, B minor.
- **Ornamentation** (trills).
- **Cadenza** on the harpsichord: this is an improvised section showing off the technical skill of the soloist.

Second Movement – Affetuoso

Time signature	C (common time)
Key signature/tonality	B minor
Form	Ritornello
Mood	Calm
Tempo	Slow

Musical features

- This movement contains the **concertino** only.
- The movements begins with the violin and flute playing in **imitation**.
- The harpsichord plays chordal accompaniment.
- Texture is **polyphonic** throughout.
- **Dotted rhythms**.
- Key change to F minor.
- **Ornamentation** (trills).

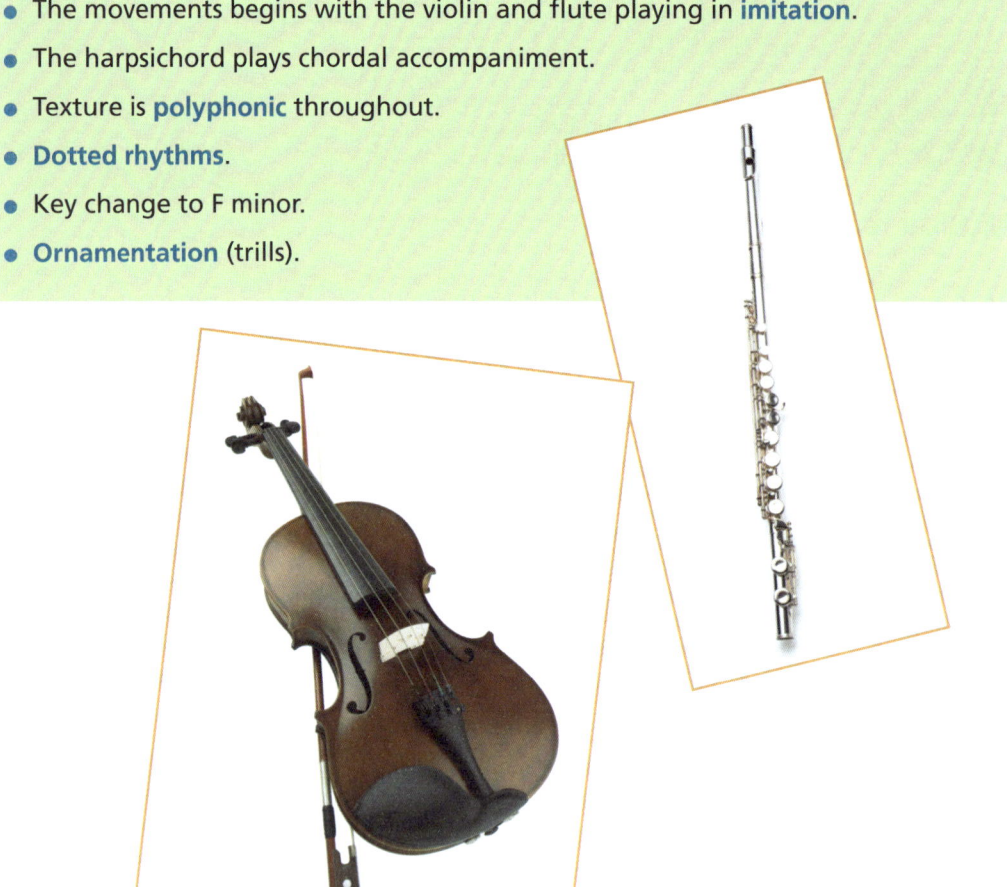

SET WORKS – QUESTION 2

Grieg's Peer Gynt Suite No. 1

- Grieg was commissioned to compose background music to Ibsen's play *Peer Gynt* in 1874.
- This work is an example of **programme music**, which sets a scene or tells a story.
- Composed in the Romantic/Naturalistic style.
- The music can also be described as **incidental music** (music written for a play).

Morning

The instruments used in this movement are as follows:

Strings	Woodwind	Brass	Percussion
Violin, viola, cello, double bass.	Flute, oboe, clarinet, bassoon.	Trumpet, horn.	Timpani.

Time signature	6/8
Key signature/tonality	E major
Form	A B A1 Coda (Ternary)
Mood	Peaceful
Tempo	Moderately fast

Musical features (Section A)

- Simple 4-bar melody alternating between **flute and oboe**.
- **Grace notes**.
- **Sequences**.
- Playing in **octaves**.
- **Strings** add to rich texture.

Musical features (Section B)

- **Cellos** play a contrasting tune.
- Contrasting **dynamics**.
- **Key changes**.

Musical features (Section A1 and Coda)

- Opening melody on **violins, oboes and bassoons**.
- Melody moves to **violins**.
- **Trills** on flutes and clarinets.
- Texture of the movement is **homophonic**.

HIGHER LEVEL QUESTION 2, 2010

Question 2: Set Works (30 marks)
An excerpt from one of your set works, played TWICE.
Answer A and B.

A

(i) This movement is called

(ii) The work from which it is taken is

(4)

B

(i) The excerpt is from
- a symphony
- incidental music
- a concerto
- an opera

(ii) Explain your choice.

(6)

Now listen to the music of bars 1–4, which is printed below.
It will be played ONCE.
Answer C.

C

(i) Which instrument plays the melody in bars 1–4?

(ii) This instrument is accompanied by
- strings only
- strings and brass
- woodwind and horn
- brass only

(6)

SET WORKS – QUESTION 2

Now listen to the music of bars 5–8 which is printed below.
It will be played ONCE.
Answer D.

D
(i) Which instrument plays the melody in bars 5–8?
_____

(ii) Briefly describe the dynamics in bars 7 and 8.
_____
(6)

Now listen to a later excerpt from the same work which is not printed here.
It will be played TWICE.
Answer E.

E
(i) Describe what you hear in this coda section by filling in the missing words.

A melody is played by _____ followed by a section featuring _____ on the clarinet and flute. Block chords are played by _____. The first melody is heard again, played by _____, and then by _____. The ending is _____.

(ii) Why is this section called a coda?
_____
_____
(8)

Anitra's Dance

The instruments used in this movement are as follows:

Strings	Percussion
Violin, viola, cello, double bass.	Triangle.

Time signature	3/4
Key signature/tonality	A minor
Form	A B A1 (Ternary)
Mood	Gentle
Tempo	Waltz-like

Musical features (Section A)

- Melody on **violins in A minor**.
- **Chromatic** melody.
- **Pizzicato** strings.
- Triangle in accompaniment.
- **Staccato** versus **arco**.
- **Ornamented** melody.

Musical features (Section B)

- New melody played in **3rds** on violins.
- **Pizzicato** versus **arco**.
- Melody repeated at higher pitch.

Musical features (Section A1)

- Opening tune returns in **D major**.
- **Imitation** between violins and violas.
- **Returns to A minor** and ends with soft chord on the strings.
- Texture of the movement is mainly **homophonic**.

In the Hall of the Mountain King

The instruments used in this movement are as follows:

Strings	Woodwind	Brass	Percussion
Violin, viola, cello, double bass.	Flute, oboe, clarinet, bassoon, piccolo.	Trumpet, trombone, horn, tuba, bass trombone.	Timpani, cymbals, bass drum.

Time signature	4/4
Key signature/tonality	B minor
Form	Theme and variation
Mood	Exciting
Tempo	March tempo

Musical features

- Based on a **melodic ostinato**.
- Theme and 18 variations.
- Begins in the bass clef and finishes in upper treble range.
- Begins softly, finishes *fff*.
- Pizz lower **strings** answered by bassoons.
- **Tempo increases** throughout the movement.
- **Staccato**.
- **Grace notes**.
- **Tremolos**.
- **Timpani roll**.
- **Homophonic** texture.

SET WORKS – QUESTION 2

Copland's Hoe-Down from *Rodeo*

- Hoe-Down is the final movement in the ballet *Rodeo*, written by Aaron Copland in 1942.
- It can be described as programme music because it tells a story.
- Written in an American style, using a fusion of 'cowboy and Western' folk music and classical music.

The instruments used in the movement are as follows:

Strings	Woodwind	Brass	Percussion
Violin, viola, cello, double bass.	Flute, piccolo, oboe, clarinet, bass clarinet, bassoon, cor anglais.	Trumpet, trombone, horn, tuba.	Timpani, xylophone, cymbals, woodblock, bass drum, snare drum, piano.

Time signature	2/4
Key signature/tonality	D major
Form	Intro A B Link A1
Mood	Lively and energetic
Tempo	Allegro (fast and lively)

Musical features (Intro)

- Lively melody played by **tutti** in D major.
- **Vamping** section on piano and woodblock.
- **Accented** notes.

Musical features (A: Bonyparte)

- A **square dance**, like a reel.
- The tune has two parts: the first part is on **strings and clarinet**; the second part on **violin, oboe and clarinet**.
- Lively **accented** tune.
- **Triplets**.

Musical features (B: McLeod's Reel)

- A new dance in **G major**.
- First part played by **trumpet and strings**.
- Second part played by **oboe, then clarinet and violin**.
- **Accented** notes.
- The section ends with a lively **syncopated** passage.

Musical features (Link)

- Like the vamping section in the Intro.
- *Rubato* (changing of tempo for expression).

Musical features (A1)

- Energetic music of the opening returns.
- Movement ends very loudly with **accented repeated notes** in the higher register.

SET WORKS – QUESTION 2

HIGHER LEVEL QUESTION 2, 2007

Question 2: Set Works (30 marks)
An excerpt from one of your set works will be played THREE times.
An outline of the music score is printed below.
Answer A, B, C and D. (Sample answers are included).

A Name the <u>movement</u> from which this excerpt is taken, and its composer.

Movement:
Hoedown

Composer:
Aaron Copland

(6)

B

(i) This excerpt is:

- the introduction
- Bonyparte
- McLeod's Reel
- the link passage

Mc Leod's Reel

(ii) The tempo is

• slow   • moderate   • fast   • varied

Fast

(4)

C

(i) The instrument that plays the melody at the beginning is the:
Trumpet

(ii) To which family does it belong?
Brass

(6)

D

(i) Name the instruments that continue the melody in bar 5.
Violins

(ii) Explain 8va in bars 16–24.
Music sounds an octave higher than written.

(6)

Now listen to a later section, which is not printed here.
You will hear it TWICE.
Answer E.

E Briefly explain what happens in this section. Refer to <u>each</u> of the following musical features: instrumentation, tempo, pitch, and dynamics.

Instrumentation:
Music is played by piano, strings, woodblock, trombone, bassoon.

Tempo:
Rubato (the music slows towards the end).

Pitch:
Pitch is low with a descending bass line.

Dynamics:
Music gets gradually softer.

(8)

Group C set works

Work	Section(s)	Composer	Date
The Four Seasons	Spring	Antonio Vivaldi	1723
L'Arlésienne Suite No. 1	Intermezzo Farandole	Georges Bizet	1872
Granuaile Suite	Ripples in the Rockpools	Shaun Davey	1985

Works recently examined:
- The Four Seasons, Spring (second movement) (2008).
- L'Arlésienne Suite – Farandole (2005).
- The Four Seasons, Spring (first movement) (2002).

Vivaldi's The Four Seasons, Spring

- An example of **programme music** that tries to illustrate the coming of spring.
- This music is composed in the Baroque style.
- **Ritornello form** is when the main theme returns many times throughout the movement. There is an **episode** (new material) between recurring instances of the main theme.
- **Homophonic** texture (**ritornello** theme) and **polyphonic** texture (**episodes**).

The instruments used in the work are as follows:

Strings	Continuo
Solo violin, string orchestra.	Cello, double bass, harpsichord.

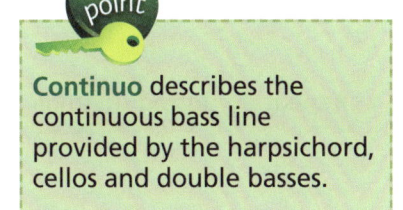

Continuo describes the continuous bass line provided by the harpsichord, cellos and double basses.

First movement – Allegro

Time signature	C (common time)
Key signature/tonality	E major
Form	Ritornello
Mood	Happy
Tempo	Allegro (fast and lively)

Musical features

- Lively **ritornello** theme played by tutti: homophonic.
- Ornamented episodes played in **counterpoint**: polyphonic.
- Trills.
- Repeated notes.
- Staccato.
- Triplets.
- Key changes to B major and C sharp minor.
- Semiquaver movement.
- Syncopation.

> **key point**
> Largo e pianissimo sempre means always slow and soft.

Second movement – Largo e pianissimo sempre

Time signature	3/4
Key signature/tonality	C sharp minor
Form	A A1
Mood	Calm and peaceful
Tempo	Very slow

Musical features

- Solo violin, two violins and viola.
- Simple triadic melody.
- Trills.
- Repeating dotted rhythmic idea.

SET WORKS – QUESTION 2

HIGHER LEVEL QUESTION 2, 2008

Question 2: Set Works (30 marks)
An excerpt from one of your set works will be played TWICE.
The melody, up to bar 18, is printed below.
Answer A, B, C, D and E. (Sample answers are included).

A
(i) Name the work from which this excerpt is taken.
Four Seasons, Spring: second movement.

(ii) The composer is
Vivaldi.
(4)

B Name **two** instruments that you hear.
1 *Solo violin.*
2 *Viola.*
(4)

C
(i) The mood of the excerpt is

- restless
- lively
- calm
- angry

Calm.

(ii) Briefly state how these features contribute to this mood:

1 Speed (tempo)
Slow.

2 Key
C sharp minor.

3 Dynamics
Soft.

(8)

D

(i) The texture is
- monophonic
- polyphonic
- homophonic

Homophonic.

(ii) Briefly explain your answer.
The melody is played with chordal accompaniment.

(4)

E

(i) Which two-note figure in the background is heard throughout?

The second pattern.

(ii) These notes:
- rise by step
- fall by step
- are repeated
- leap an octave

Are repeated.

(4)

Now listen to an excerpt from a different movement, which is not printed here. You will hear it TWICE.
Answer F.

F Briefly define three of the following terms that are associated with this excerpt.

1 Programme music
Music that tells a story.

2 Concerto
A piece for a solo instrument(s) and orchestra.

3 Ritornello
A section that keeps returning.

4 Continuo
Keyboard instrument (harpsichord) usually with cello.

(6)

Bizet's L'Arlésienne Suite No. 1

- This is an example of **incidental music** (music written for a play).
- It is composed in the **Romantic** style.
- A **suite** is a collection of dances or pieces of music.
- An **intermezzo** is a piece of music that is played between the acts of a play.
- A **farandole** is a lively French dance from the area of Provence.

The instruments used in this work are as follows:

Strings	Woodwind	Brass	Percussion
Violin, viola, cello, double bass, harp.	Flute, oboe, clarinet, bassoon, cor anglais, saxophone.	Horn, cornet.	Timpani.

Second movement – Intermezzo

Time signature	4/4
Key signature/tonality	E flat major
Form	A B A1 (Ternary)
Mood	Solemn
Tempo	Broad and slow

Musical features (A)

- **Accented** melody.
- Much **quieter** answering phrase.
- Ends with a **perfect cadence**.

Musical features (B)

- More **lyrical** melody on saxophone, cornet and clarinet.
- Arpeggic accompaniment.
- Harp joins in.
- Section ends loudly with accented notes.

Musical features (A1)

- **Accented** melody returns.
- **Tremolo**.
- Ends with tutti playing accented loud notes.
- **Perfect cadence**.
- Texture is **homophonic** throughout.

Fourth movement – Farandole

Time signature	4/4, 2/4
Key signature/tonality	D minor/D major
Form	A B A&B Binary
Mood	Lively
Tempo	Fast; very fast; and lively

Musical features (A, March)

- Opening melody in D minor, played by **tutti**.
- Opening melody is **homophonic** and the dynamic is *ff*.
- It is repeated in **canon** (imitation at a fixed distance), **polyphonic**.

Musical features (B, Dance)

- Changes to **D major**.
- Time changes to **2/4** and the dynamic is *pppp*.
- Tambourine, followed by **staccato melody on flute and clarinet**.
- Key change to **B minor**.
- **Homophonic** texture.

Musical features (March & Dance)

- Each tune heard alternately and then together in **counterpoint** (two independent melodies played together), **polyphonic**.
- Begins in **B minor**.
- Changes to **D major**, gets **louder**.
- Ends with the **dance tune** in D major, **exciting finish**.

Shaun Davey's Ripples in the Rockpools

- This piece is a fusion of Irish traditional music and modern classical/orchestral music.
- It is the second movement from the suite Granuaile by Shaun Davey.

The instruments used in the work are as follows:

Strings	Woodwind	Brass	Percussion	Other	Voices
Violin, viola, cello, double bass.	Flute, oboe, clarinet, bassoon.	Horn, trumpet.	Timpani, conga drums, xylophone.	Uilleann pipes, harp, guitar.	Male and female soloists.

Time signature	Changing: 4/4; 7/8; 2/4; 3/8; 5/4
Key signature/tonality	Re mode
Form	Verses and instrumental
Mood	Lively
Tempo	Fast; very fast; and lively

Musical features

- Two-bar intro of **repeated notes** on violas.
- Verse sung by female soloist, accompanied by guitar, violas and cellos.
- Melody based on **4-note** idea.
- **Changing time signatures**.
- **Harmony** introduced in **chorus**.
- Short musical interlude before next verse.
- **Imitation of wind** by flute and clarinet (**word painting**).
- **Reel** on uilleann pipes.
- **Harp glissando** leads to repeat of chorus.
- Ends abruptly.

Granuaile, Michael Cooper—statue situated on the grounds of Westport House, Co. Mayo, Ireland.

7 Irish Traditional Music – Question 3

aims
- To learn about Irish traditional music: its instruments, dance tunes, styles and characteristics.
- To develop a knowledge of the history and recent developments of Irish music.

Question 3 is worth **40 marks** or a total of **10%** of the whole exam.

What the syllabus says …
All candidates must show some knowledge of Irish traditional music and:

- Its unique features and the characteristics of different types of performances.
- A general account of its history and some awareness of its growth in popularity today.
- Irish traditional instruments (aural recognition).

You must be able to:

- Identify a variety of dance styles.
- Identify the dance's time signatures and typical bars of rhythm.
- Identify vocal styles and characteristics.

IRISH TRADITIONAL MUSIC – QUESTION 3

You must also have some knowledge of:

- Irish traditional musical characteristics and history, instruments and collectors.
- Past and ongoing developments and styles in Irish traditional music.
- Fusion with other musical styles.

There are usually **three different listening excerpts** and each excerpt is played **twice**. Over the past few years these excerpts have usually been:

1. A traditional dance form (jig, reel, hornpipe, etc.).
2. A sean nós or folk song.
3. An interesting type of modern music: a fusion of Irish traditional music features and modern pop/rock/folk/ethnic or other styles.

Typical exam questions include:

- Name the melody instruments and the harmony/rhythm instruments in this extract.
- Name the type of dance being played.
- Write/circle a bar of typical rhythm/time signature.
- What traditional (or non-traditional) features can you hear in this excerpt?
- What style of singing can you hear?
- Questions on musicality (form, accompaniment, performers, etc.) based on the excerpts.

Sometimes you must also answer an essay-type question, usually part D of Question 3, based on your studies of Irish traditional music:

- 2010 – Higher level: One collector.
- 2009 – Higher level: Role of the harper, Belfast Harp Festival.
- 2008 – Higher level: Irish traditional instruments.
- 2007 – Higher level: Two organisations that have helped traditional music become popular today.
- 2006 – Higher level: Traditional instruments.
- 2005 – Higher level: Preservation of Irish music (collectors).
- 2004 – Higher level: Write a note on a solo or group performance.
- 2003 – Higher level: Collector or solo performer.
- 2002 – Higher level: Sean nós performance.
- 2001 – Higher level: Irish folk songs.

Other topics may include:

- Musicians (groups or solo artists) who use fusion in their performance.
- The harp tradition in Ireland.
- Irish dance tunes.
- General characteristics of Irish traditional music.
- Contemporary Irish composers who are influenced by traditional music.

History of Irish traditional music: Quick revision

Medieval – early seventeenth century
Irish society consisted of the nobility, the commoners and the professional learned class, including the **file** (poet) and the **reacaire** (harpist).

Two traditions: seventeenth and eighteenth centuries
The fiddlers, pipers and ballad singers thrived in this era and represented the cultural musical tradition of most Irish people. The musical traditions of the 'Big Houses' and the middle class inside the Pale were becoming more influenced by Italian classical music, including operas and oratorios. The **Belfast Harp Festival of 1792** was organised to 'revive and perpetuate the Ancient Music and Poetry of Ireland'.

Emigration and the deterioration of Irish music culture in the nineteenth century

The Famine and the mass emigration that resulted from it brought about a decline in musicians, dance masters and the use of the Irish language. Much traditional folklore was lost in Ireland, but traditional Irish music became part of the fabric of life from the US to Australia.

The revival of Irish traditional music in the twentieth century

With Irish independence a new breed of traditional musician was born: one who could revive old folklore and interpret it for the world of the twentieth century. The formation of céilí bands, radio and television programmes and recordings, Seán Ó Riada and his Comhaltas Ceoltóirí Éireann (CCÉ), and the fusion of Irish traditional music with pop and many other styles of music all promoted Irish traditional music all over the world.

Musical features

1. In past eras (pre-twentieth century), singers were usually **unaccompanied** (usually no harmony, apart from drones). Nowadays harmony (guitar, piano, vocal harmony, etc.) can be an important part of many traditional styles.
2. Ornamentation (grace notes, slides, turns, rolls, replacing long notes with repeated notes and cuts) is often used in many types of Irish traditional music.
3. Tempo, dynamics and other musical expressive effects are not normally used in traditional music. One mood for each tune, and usually one key per tune, with no modulation.
4. Traditional music was usually a **solo** art form, but nowadays it is usually performed by groups or ensembles.
5. Most Irish traditional dance music is in a major key (tonality) but minor and modal (modes and gapped scales) are also found, especially in traditional singing (sean nós).
6. Melodies (both dance melodies and sung melodies, usually in the treble clef) have a wide range.
7. The last note of a dance tune is sometimes repeated at the end of each phrase or the end of the piece.
8. Irish traditional music is an **aural tradition**, passed on and taught by ear. Nowadays, many traditional songs and dances are written down so they are accessible to musicians all over the world.
9. The texture of most Irish traditional dance music is now **homophonic** (melody with accompaniment) whereas it originally was monophonic. It is rarely, if ever, polyphonic.

10 Many different instruments (e.g. accordions, fiddle) have been absorbed into Irish traditional music over the centuries and are now just as important as the likes of the Irish harp and uillean pipes.

11 Non-traditional instruments (e.g. guitar, banjo, bass guitar and drum kits) are very common today in the performance of Irish traditional music, as they are for the **fusion** styles of a mixture of pop/rock/classical/folk/African music with Irish traditional music.

Instruments

The core instruments used in Irish traditional music are:

- Irish harp – pre-tenth century.
- Fiddle – used in Irish music from the seventeenth century.
- Uillean pipes – early eighteenth century.
- Flute – eighteenth century.
- Accordion (button and piano) – twentieth century.
- Concertina – 1850s.
- Melodeon – end of nineteenth century.
- Bodhrán.
- Whistles (tin whistles, low whistles).
- Bones and spoons.

Non-traditional instruments used nowadays in recordings, concerts and sessions include: guitar, banjo, piano, harmonica, bouzouki and many types of synthesised sounds.

IRISH TRADITIONAL MUSIC – QUESTION 3

> **key point**
>
> **Identifying the melody instrument** in a traditional musical excerpt can be quite difficult.
>
> Uillean pipes and their **drones** are easy to recognise, but accordions/fiddles, flutes/whistles, guitar/banjo/bouzouki are harder to hear and distinguish because sometimes many instruments play just the melody line. **Listen to recordings** to help you analyse the **timbre** (tone colour) of each instrument. In a group session, like a céilí band, you may hear the piano vamping or a basic drum kit keeping the beat (snare and bass drum).

SOME FAMOUS IRISH TRADITIONAL MUSICIANS AND INSTRUMENTALISTS:

- Harp – Derek Bell.
- Uilleann pipes – Séamus Ennis, Paddy Maloney, Davy Spillane, Liam Ó Floinn, Paddy Keenan.
- Fiddle – Michael Coleman, James Morrison, Frankie Gavin, Paddy Glacken, Mairéad Ní Mhaonaigh, Martin Hayes.
- Button accordion – Joe Cooley, Sharon Shannon.
- Flute – Matt Molloy, Séamus Tansey.
- Tin whistle – Seán Potts, Mary Bergin.
- Mandolin/bouzouki – Dónal Lunny, Andy Irvine.

Traditional Irish dance tunes

1. Dance tunes are the **most common** traditional Irish music played.

2. Most tunes come from the **eighteenth and nineteenth centuries**.

3. Many dances were influenced by similar European dances.

4. **Jigs, reels, hornpipes** and **polkas** are the most common dance tunes found in the traditional repertoire.

5. Other forms include mazurkas and slides, and highlands, barn dances and set and céilí dance sets.

6. Rhythm and 'swing' are the most important features of dance music.

7. Most dance tunes are in a **simple repeated binary (AB) form**; usually consisting of A (8-bar phrases) repeated, B repeated. Either or both of these phrases may be repeated again.

8. The tune can then run straight into another dance, producing a longer 'set' of dance tunes.

9. **Set dances** were created by the dancing masters of the eighteenth and nineteenth centuries. These tunes are usually set to slow jigs or hornpipe rhythms.

10. **Slow airs** are often the instrumental rendition of the melodies (laments), or 'airs' of songs, usually sean nós songs.

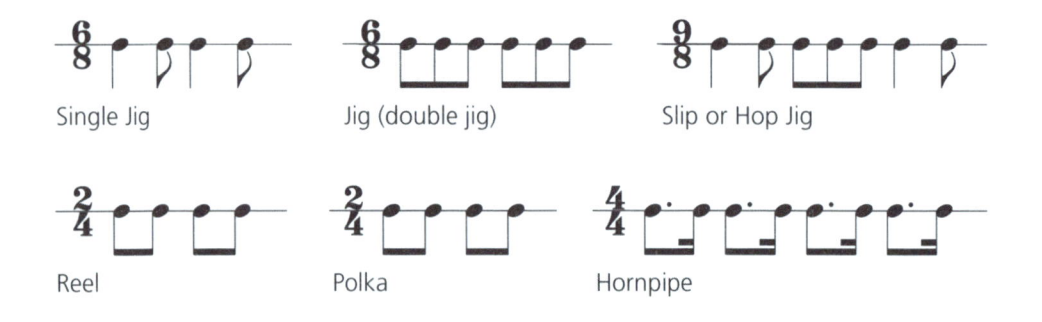

Single Jig

Jig (double jig)

Slip or Hop Jig

Reel

Polka

Hornpipe

Dance type	Tempo	Time signature	Origin	Features
Single jig	Fast	6/8	England	Crotchet/quaver rhythm
Double jig	Fast	6/8		Quaver rhythm ('rashers and sausages')
Slip/hop jig	Moderate	9/8		Mixture of crotchets and quavers ('rashers and sizzling sausages')
Reel	Fast	2/4, 4/4	Scotland	Running quavers ('black and decker')
Polka	Fast 2 per bar	2/4	Bohemia	Strong rythm
Hornpipe	Steady 4 per bar	4/4	England	Accented dotted rythm

The performance of Irish traditional dancing has **flourished in the past 50 years**. **Worldwide appreciation** of this art form, which emphasises technique, speed of step and costumes, has grown with national and international Irish dancing competitions. In recent years, Irish music has enjoyed increasing popularity worldwide, largely as a result of wildly successful, internationally performed dance and music stage extravaganzas such as *Riverdance* and *Lord of the Dance*, as well as the 'steerage scene' from the movie *Titanic*.

The Irish harp

- There are two types of Irish harp:
  1. Ancient Celtic (Gaelic) harp.
  2. Neo-Irish harp.
- The Irish for harp is *cruit* or *cláirseach*.
- Aristocratic instrument played by professional harpers from the fifteenth to the eighteenth centuries.
- A *planxty* is a piece of music for harp (usually honouring some patron or chieftain).

Celtic or Gaelic harp	Neo-Irish harp
22 strings: bronze or wire	34/36 strings: gut or nylon
Plucked by fingernails	Played with fingertips
Resonant, rich, bell-like tone	Softer, gentler tone
Strings need to be dampened	Sound does note vibrate for long
Based on drones in F and G; tuned approximately in B flat	Tuned in C (diatonic)
Made from bogwood	Invented by John Egan. A smaller version of the concert harp but without pedals
Melody played on lower strings by the right hand	Melody played in treble by right hand, left hand
Performers: Turlough O'Carolan; Denis Hempson	Performer: Laoise Kelly

Turlough O'Carolan (1670–1738)

- Ireland's most famous **harper**, his music is very popular and is played by musicians on a variety of instruments.
- In his music we hear an assortment of styles, from early modal Celtic melodies to airs and planxties, from early dance music to neo-classical Italian-influenced Baroque compositions.
- Composed his music on the traditional Irish harp at a time when that instrument was beginning to decline in popularity. The long sustains of the brass strings on that instrument produces a sound very different from that heard on today's neo-Irish harp.

The 1792 Belfast Harp Festival

- In July 1792, ten Irish harpers competed at the Belfast Harp Festival for the first prize of ten guineas. They included Denis Hampson and Arthur O'Neill.
- The first prize was awarded to Charles Fanning for 'An Cuilfionn'.
- In all, the ten harpers played forty tunes.

Edward Bunting – collectors of Irish music

- Bunting was a nineteen-year-old classically-trained professional musician in Belfast when he was engaged at the Harp Festival of 1792 to write down the music of the harpers.
- He made the collection, arrangement and publication of traditional music his life work.
- He published three volumes of airs – the *General Collection of the Ancient Irish Music* – in 1796, 1807 and 1840, which made him famous.
- He also collected or was given more than 500 unpublished traditional song texts, most of them in the Irish language, which were rediscovered in 1907 and are now in the library of Queen's University, Belfast.

The Irish song tradition

The Irish song tradition is diverse and rich. There are different styles of singing and different styles of song. Styles include:

1. **Sean nós style**
2. **Ballad/folk style – in Irish, English or a mixture of both languages (macaronic).**

Styles of song include:

- Love songs (geantraí).
- Laments (goltraí).
- Lullabies (suantraí).
- Aislings and patriotic songs.
- Work songs and play songs.
- Religious songs and carols.
- Drinking songs.
- Humorous songs.

exam focus

Make sure you are familiar with the **names of different types of songs**. It is easy to find the most common songs on YouTube or iTunes. Have a look and a listen.

Characteristics of Sean Nós singing

This '**old style**' of traditional singing is unique to Ireland. It is a highly skilled solo art form that dates back many centuries. Themes and stories in the songs are usually about human life: birth, love, suffering, emigration and death.

1. **Solo singing – unaccompanied.**
2. Usually no dynamics, expression and little vibrato employed.
3. The most important thing is the words and the story – the rhythm of the song is dictated by the speech and syllable patterns.
4. Often there is an emphasis on the consonants *l*, *m* and *r* to facilitate the free rhythmic pulse and to create a drone effect.
5. Both Irish and English language songs in existence, even some with a mixture of both languages (macaronic).
6. Emotion is expressed through the use of vocal ornamentation, which varies from singer to singer and place to place.
7. Not much repetition in songs (through-composed).
8. The use of the glottal stop/dramatic pause.
9. Modal scales often used.
10. A nasal tone quality (nasalisation) is sometimes used.
11. No strict tempo – free rhythm and *rubato* tempo.
12. Melismatic singing – using many notes to one syllable, usually on an important word.
13. Slow airs, played in imitation of sean nós songs, are also played with very loose time signatures.

Each singer may have their own unique style but there are three regional styles country-wide:

Ulster style:
- Smaller range of song, Scots Gaelic influence.
- Little ornamentation, nasal style, steadier pulse.
- Lilis O'Laoire

Connaught style:
- Lots of ornamentation and decoration.
- More complex forms of singing.
- Seosamh O'hEanaí

Munster style:
- More like classical singing.
- Wider range in songs.
- Some ornamentation used.
- Nicolas Toíbín

Other Sean nós singers: Tríona Ní Dhomhnaill, Nóirín Ní Riain, Jack MacDhonnacha, Liam Ó Maonlaí and Paddy Tunney.

Many traditional Irish songs are not sean nós-style songs. Many hundreds of folk songs and ballads have been passed down from generation to generation over the past two centuries. Dance tunes are sometimes '**lilted**', that is, sung with **nonsense syllables**. Many composed folk songs and ballads of the 1960s and 1970s have also become incorporated into this tradition.

- A huge variety of modern traditional styles can be said to come under this heading of 'traditional songs', from the rebel songs of The Dubliners to Mary Black's popular ballads to Liam Ó Maonlaí's imaginative vocal fusion.
- There are also many songs such as 'Down by the Sally Gardens' and 'The Londonderry Air', which were collected and later arranged for classical singing with piano accompaniment (by the likes of Thomas Moore).

Fusion

- Fusion is a **mixture** of styles from different musical traditions.
- Irish traditional music has been fused with many different styles of music: jazz, pop, classical and rock. Other genres of fusion can be of a mixture of African drumming and traditional Irish dance music or Aboriginal didgeridoo droning and sean nós singing, for example.
- These styles are easy to define and analyse: each has separate definite musical characteristics in both traditions.
- But sometimes it is difficult to say why some music sounds 'Irish' or 'Celtic', because it may not have any obvious defining Irish traditional musical characteristics.
- The term 'Celtic music' usually combines Irish traditional music with various other types of traditional music, including music from Scotland, Canada, Wales, northern England, Brittany in northwest France, and sometimes Galicia in northwestern Spain.
- One group that used a fusion of Irish traditional music and rock was Horslips.

HORSLIPS

- Founded in Dublin in 1970.
- **Members:** Jim Lockhart, Barry Devlin, Johnny Fean, Eamon Carr and Charles O'Connor.
- **Instruments:** fiddle, uilleann pipes, whistles, banjo, bodhrán, flutes, mandolin and concertina; also electric and acoustic guitars, bass guitar, keyboards and drums.
- **Style: Celtic rock.** A fusion of traditional, country, folk and rock styles. Horslips mainly used Irish dance tunes, slow airs and old planxties in a rock style. Many of their albums were based on Irish myths. Used a mixture of English and Irish language in their songs. 'Dearg Doom' and 'King of the Fairies' were number 1 singles for Horslips, who were very popular in the 1970s and toured widely in the US and Europe.

Famous Irish performers and composers

Traditional groups	Solo performers	Solo singers	Fusion groups	Composers
The Chieftains	Sharon Shannon	Mary Black	Horslips	Mícheál Ó Súilleabháin
Planxty	Dónal Lunny	Dolores Keane	Hothouse Flowers	Bill Whelan
Altan	Christy Moore	Liam Ó Maonlaí	Moving Hearts	Shaun Davey
The Dubliners	Liam Ó Floinn	Paul Brady	The Corrs	Seán Ó Riada
De Danann	Niall Keegan	Christy Moore	Clannad	Michael McGlynn

Traditional terminology

Bodhrán – simple frame drum, made with goat skin, beaten with a double-sided stick or the hand (fingers or knuckles).
CCÉ (Comhaltas Ceoltóirí Éireann) – a club set up in 1951 to promote Irish traditional music and dancing.
Céilí – a social occasion for traditional dancing.
Collector – a person or institution (RTÉ, BBC) who notates (and nowadays records) the music and words of traditional music, songs and dances. This is a vital role in sustaining a living aural tradition and preserving a historical tradition.
Fleadh Cheoil – the biggest annual festival of Irish traditional music with street sessions, classes in music, singing and dancing, concerts and competitions. Run by Comhaltas Ceoltóirí Éireann.
Hiberno-jazz – a fusion of traditional Irish music with jazz characteristics.
Lilting – singing a tune using nonsense words.
Sean nós – old style of Irish traditional singing.
Session – a group or gathering of traditional musicians (and/or singers) to participate in music making and fun.
Vamping – a type of piano accompaniment used in traditional music; the pianist usually plays a simple chordal accompaniment.

IRISH TRADITIONAL MUSIC – QUESTION 3

HIGHER LEVEL QUESTION 3, 2009

Question 3: Irish Music (40 marks)
THREE excerpts, each played TWICE.
Answer A, B and C.

A Excerpt 1

(i) Name this dance.
_____

(ii) The time signature is
_____

(iii) The rhythm pattern is

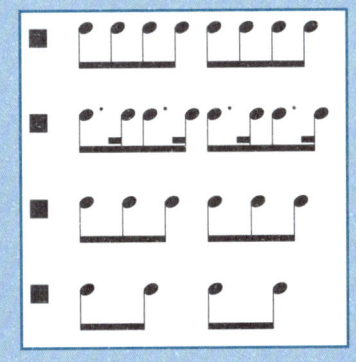

_____
(9)

B Excerpt 2

(i) This style of singing is called
_____

(ii) List **two** traditional features of this performance.
   1 _____
   2 _____

(iii) Comment on **one** unusual feature.
_____
(11)

C Excerpt 3

(i) Name **three** different melody instruments that play in this excerpt.
   1 _____
   2 _____
   3 _____

(ii) The accompaniment plays mainly
- a countermelody
- broken chords
- block chords
- scale passages

_____

(11)

Now answer D. *(There is no music on the recording here).*

D

(i) What was the role of the harper in Ireland in the past?
_____
_____
_____
_____

(ii) Describe the 1792 event that helped to preserve harp music.
_____
_____
_____
_____
_____
_____

(9)

8 Melodic and Rhythmic Dictation – Question 4

aims
- To develop a confident, step-by-step approach to the melodic and rhythmic dictation on the exam paper.

- Melodic and Rhythmic Dictation – Higher level. **HL**
- Rhythmic Dictation – Ordinary level.

Question 4 is worth **40 marks**.

exam focus

In most cases there will be a **dotted crotchet-quaver rhythm** in the dictation question. This can occur in any bar, but most usually appears in bar 2 or bar 3. It usually ends on **doh (tonic note)** with a fairly long note value. Don't forget to **write in your barlines**, using a double bar at the end. Getting the rhythm correct will only gain you around 15 of the 40 marks! Make an attempt at the **pitch**.

Read all parts of the question carefully. In 1995, a five-bar phrase was played, not a four-bar phrase – which really confused many candidates who didn't read the question!

You can use either:
1. Staff notation (most candidates answer in this way).
2. Tonic solfa (very few candidates understand this form of notation); or
3. A combination of staff notation and tonic solfa.

Melodic dictation
Higher level Question 4.
- Use a sharp B pencil.
- Be as neat as possible.

key point

You are usually given the exact number of notes that you must fill in on the stave. Don't forget to go back and **double check** when you have finished notating your answer.

HL

1. Read **all** instructions carefully.

2. **Check the key** (you could even write out the scale for reference).

3. Put in **barlines**, including a double barline at the end.

4. **Concentrate** intently on the whole phrase.

5. After the **first two hearings, you should have a good idea of the full rhythm**. Don't forget to listen for the dotted crotchet-quaver rhythm and count how long the final note is.

6. By the end of the **third hearing, you should be able to sing back the phrase** (*in your head!*). Does it end on doh? Can you discover any interval leaps, repeating notes or patterns? Can you draw a melodic line (song map) of the movement of the melody?

7. During the **fourth hearing, you should concentrate on the first pitch after the last given note** (usually in bar 1). It is vital that you get this note correct. Did it repeat any note already given? Did it move up or down by step, or stay static? Did it jump? If so, up or down? How far?

8. **After the fourth hearing try to finish writing the pitches of the melody**, especially the lead-in to the final note (think of a final cadence and the notes that might be used).

9. **The final hearing should be used for checking back over the dictation.**

10. Don't ever rub anything out if you are not absolutely sure it is wrong!

11. Go back though your answer and double check every rhythmic value, note, and even direction of stem.

There are many different ways of training your ear to hear and dictate melodies and rhythm patterns. **Solfa** is one of the most common ways of becoming a fantastic sight-singer and becoming very good at Question 4.

Solfa

Solfa (solfege) is a set of syllables that represent pitch or relationships between pitches in music. The syllables are: ***doh, re, mi, fah, soh, la, ti*** and then ***doh*** again, one octave above the original ***doh*** (tonic note).

Hand signs are a way of giving a physical placement for a vocal pitch. The low 'doh' begins at your midsection. Each pitch is then above the previous one. Thus, you have the hand signs going up when the pitch goes up. The upper 'doh' is at eye level.

What is relative solfa?

In relative solfa every **major** scale is sung to the sound doh, re, mi, fah, soh, la, ti, doh; while every (natural) **minor** scale is sung to the sound la, ti, doh, re, mi, fah, soh, la.

Song mapping

This can be a good **visual tool** if you are not great at identifying interval leaps but are fine at notating the rhythm! A song map or music map is a line that represents the flow or movement of the melody, in an ascending, descending or static line. Draw the line while you are listening to the dictation excerpt (probably for the third or fourth time, assuming that you have a good rhythmic outline). This map is a kinaesthetic symbol as well as a visual one.

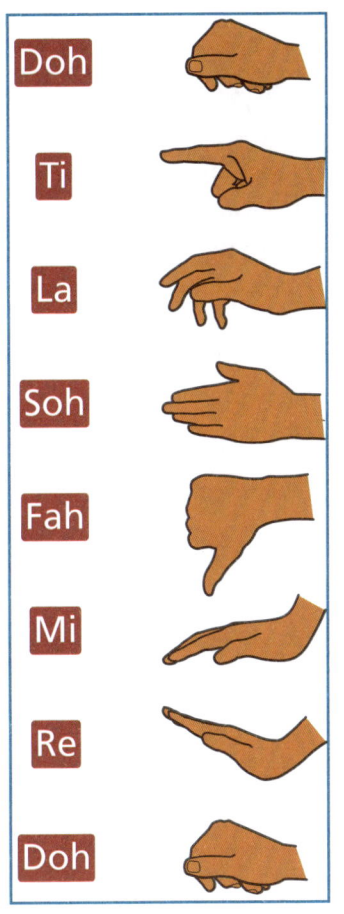

Rhythm dotting

Rhythm dots are made by (quietly) **tapping the rhythm of the dictation pattern with the tip of your pencil above the empty bars, leaving a visual record of the note movement.** Each dot represents a single sound. The idea is to hear the individual rhythm sounds of the dictation excerpt. This is a fast method of **identifying rhythm patterns** for students who are good at this difficult question. Other candidates use stick notation or make up their own way of identifying minims, crotchets, etc. in shorthand.

Key signatures

The key signatures used for the dictation question are very accessible.
- D major – 2010, 2007, 2005, 2003 – all in 4/4 time.
- G major – 2006 (3/4 time); 2004, 2002 – 4/4 time.
- F major – 2008, 2001 – 4/4 time.
- C major – 2009 – 4/4 time.

But you still need to understand how to notate correctly in or on lower or higher ledger lines.

HIGHER LEVEL QUESTION 4, 2010

Question 4: Dictation (40 marks)
A FOUR-BAR PHRASE, played FIVE times on the piano.
There will be an appropriate pause after each playing.
The keynote and the tonic chord will be sounded before each playing.
You will hear the **pulse** on the metronome before and during the **first two playings only**.
To help you, the **first four notes** are given.
Answer A, B and C.

A	Add the remaining 10 MELODY NOTES.	(20)
B	Write the RHYTHM PATTERN.	(16)
C	Put in the BARLINES.	(4)

Use **one** of the three options below:

I: Staff notation

OR

II: Tonic solfa [doh = D]

d : m | s : m

OR

III: A combination of stick (or other) notation and tonic solfa

4/4 d   m   s   m

9 Choice Songs and Choice Works – Question 5

aims
- To be able to name a piece of music from each of the categories in this question.
- To know some musical features of the chosen pieces.
- To develop general listening skills through aural recognition of various aspects of the music.

Question 5 is worth **40 marks**.

For the first part of this question (*which is usually only worth 10 marks out of the 40*) you need to know at least **one** piece from **each** of the eight different song categories and **one** piece from **each** of the six different choice works categories. **The remaining questions, worth 30 marks**, or 10% of the total listening paper, are typically based around general aural-musicianship skills related to a previously unheard song or work.

You need to study at least **one** piece from **each** of the following categories of choice songs and choice works. That is at least **14 pieces** (**eight songs** and **six works minimum**) – and you will probably be only examined on one choice song or choice work.

> **The syllabus states that:**
> Candidates are required to select a minimum of **TWELVE** further songs for special study, at least **ONE** of which must be taken from each of the prescribed categories. For each piece you must know the **name, composer, relevant background information** and **musical characteristics**.
> **Note: Do not write on your set song or set work here!**

Categories

Choice song categories
(These are the same as the set song categories!)

1. Traditional Irish songs.
2. Folk songs from other countries.
3. Art songs.

4. Historical and modern ballads.

5. Popular songs including spirituals, jazz and blues songs.

6. Vocal church music and carols.

7. Songs from operas, musicals, cantatas and oratorios.

8. Songs involving simple descants, ostinati, simple two-part songs, rounds and canons.

Can you find a choice song that can fit into more than one category?

Choice work categories

1. **Dance movements**.

2. One **symphonic movement** from either a classical symphony or a symphonic suite, or any orchestral work that utilises Irish traditional or popular elements.

3. **Theme and variations** in the classical or Irish repertoire, or a jazz movement.

4. A movement involving a **soloist** (instrumental or vocal) or a group of soloists or choir **with accompaniment**.

5. **Illustrative** or **film** music.

6. **Concert overtures, preludes** or **intermezzi** from musicals, plays, operas, operettas or oratorios.

CHOICE SONGS AND CHOICE WORKS – QUESTION 5

> **key point**
>
> Relevant **background information** on the chosen works and their composers, as well as the **origins and aspects of the usual orchestral forms** (see Chapter 16) will also be required.

> **exam focus**
>
> The following categories have appeared in recent years:
>
> - 2010 – Choice Work: a movement involving an instrumental or vocal soloist or a group of soloists or choir interacting with an accompanying ensemble.
> - 2009 – Choice Work: illustrative or film music.
> - 2008 – Choice Songs: songs composed by the great masters and recognised twentieth-century composers.
> - 2007 – Choice Work: a movement involving a soloist with accompaniment.
> - 2006 – Choice Songs: songs from operas, musicals, cantatas, etc.
> - 2005 – Choice Work: illustrative or film music.
> - 2004 – Choice Work: theme and variations.
> - 2003 – Choice Songs: historical modern ballads.
> - 2002 – Choice Works: overtures, preludes and intermezzi.
> - 2001 – Choice Work: illustrative or film music.

Aural skills questions

These questions are designed, through aural recognition, to test your knowledge of general listening skills (see Understanding Musical Features, p. 11).

You **must** be able to listen to the extracts and give a variety of explanatory answers on the excerpt's main musical features:

- Origins.
- Similarities and differences.
- Changes in mood.
- Tempo.
- Tonality.
- Time signature.
- General stylistic features and the varying components of musical texture, timbre, performing forces, pitch, etc.

LESS STRESS MORE SUCCESS

The music in these excerpts covers many different musical styles. You should, after **actively listening** to many different types of music, both in music lessons and out of class, be able to answer these questions using proper musical terminology (Italian, English or even German). If you can't think of a suitable technical term, try to explain your ideas fully, clearly and concisely, referring to the musical excerpt given.

> **key point**
> When describing a **personal response** to a particular piece of music or its performance, use descriptive words like colourful, energetic, busy, restful, inspiring, dance-like, etc. **Don't** leave blank spaces or empty lines. **Don't** use one-word answers when you're asked for an explanation, description or comparison between two excerpts. For example, if you're asked to compare or contrast two musical features in different excerpts, to gain full marks you must mention **both** excerpts for **each** feature.

> **exam focus**
> Download some podcasts from www.rte.ie/lyricfm and listen to some opera, choral, world music or contemporary music from RTÉ's classical music station.

Create a grid of your **choice works**, using the template below as a guide:

Category	Name of Choice Work	Composer and Country	Musical Features and Terms
Dance movements	Can can from Orpheus in the underworld	Jacques Offenbach	
Symphonic movements			
Theme and variations	When the saints go marching in	Louis Armstrong	Syncopation, call and answer
Soloist and accompaniment			
Illustrative/film music			
Overtures, etc.			

Create a grid of your **choice songs**, using the template below as a guide:

Category	Name of Choice Song	Composer and Country	Musical Features and Terms
Irish folk songs			
Folk songs from other countries			
Art songs			
Historical and modern ballads			
Popular songs, spirituals, jazz songs			
Church music/carols			
Songs from opera, musicals, cantatas, oratorios			
Two-part songs, rounds, canons			

CHOICE SONGS AND CHOICE WORKS – QUESTION 5

HIGHER LEVEL QUESTION 5, 2010

Question 5: Chosen Songs and Works (40 marks)
A movement involving an instrumental or vocal soloist or a group of soloists or choir interacting with an accompanying ensemble

Answer A and B. (There is no music on the recording for these sections).

A Name your CHOSEN WORK in this category and its COMPOSER. (Do NOT name your set works: Brandenburg Concerto No. 5, Peer Gynt Suite or 'Hoe-Down' from Rodeo here).

(i) Chosen work: _____

(ii) Composer: _____

(4)

B State why your chosen work is suitable for this category and briefly describe <u>one</u> musical feature of the work.
_____
_____

(5)

You will now hear an excerpt from a work that you may not have heard before. It will be played TWICE.
Answer C and D.

C

(i) The opening *instrumental* section contains
- Long held notes
- Ascending scales
- Descending scales
- Repeated notes

_____

(ii) Briefly explain your choice.
_____
_____
_____

(5)

D

(i) The choir consists of
- male voices only
- female voices only
- male and female voices

(ii) Name the brass instruments heard for the first time as the choir starts singing.

(iii) Name the percussion instruments.

(9)

You will now hear another excerpt from the same work.
It will be played ONCE.
Answer E.

E

(i) The texture of the music is
- homophonic
- monophonic
- polyphonic

(ii) Briefly explain your choice.

(5)

You will now hear both excerpts again played ONCE only.
Answer F.

F Compare the two extracts under <u>three</u> of the following: mood, speed, time signature and rhythm.

	Excerpt 1	Excerpt 2
Mood		
Speed		
Time signature		
Rhythm		

(12)

CHOICE SONGS AND CHOICE WORKS – QUESTION 5

HIGHER LEVEL QUESTION 5, 2008

Question 5: Chosen Songs and Works (40 marks)

Songs composed by the great masters and recognised twentieth-century composers.

Answer A and B. (There is no music on the recording for these sections).

A Name your CHOSEN SONG in this category, and its COMPOSER.
(Do NOT name your set song 'Caro Mio Ben' ('Come Happy Spring') here').

(i) Chosen song: _____

(ii) Composer: _____

(4)

B Identify and briefly describe one musical feature of this song.

Feature: _____

Description: _____

(6)

You will now hear the beginning of a song by Mahler played THREE times. The words and translation are printed below.

1. Ging heut' morgen übers Feld,	I walked across the fields this morning.
2. Tau noch auf den Gräsern hing;	Dew still hung on every blade of grass.
3. Sprach zu mir der lust'ge Fink:	The merry finch spoke to me:
4. 'Ei du! Gelt?	'Hey! Isn't it?
5. Guten Morgen!	Good morning!
6. Ei gelt? Du! Wird's nicht eine schöne Welt?	Isn't it? You! Doesn't it become a fine world?
7. Zink! Zink! Schön und flink!	Chirp! Chirp! Fair and sharp!
8. Wie mir doch die Welt gefällt!"	How the world delights me!'

Answer C and D.

C

(i) The singer is
 • a tenor   • an alto   • a soprano   • a bass

(ii) The accompaniment is played on
 • a guitar   • a harpsichord   • a piano   • an organ

(6)

D

(i) In line 1, the melody features
- triplets
- changing time signature
- a descending scale
- an ascending scale

(ii) In lines 2, 3 and 4, the melody in the accompaniment plays with the voice in
- unison
- harmony
- octaves
- imitation

(iii) Outline any **one** point of interest in the accompaniment from line 7 to the end.

(8)

You will now hear the closing section of the song, in a different performance, played TWICE.
Answer E.

E

(i) The instrument which extends the singer's opening phrase is
- a French horn
- a violin
- an oboe
- a bassoon

(ii) The first and second phrases are sung as a sequence. Explain this term as you hear it in the recording.

(8)

You will now hear both excerpts played ONCE only.
Answer F.

F Identify <u>two</u> similarities and <u>two</u> differences between excerpt one and excerpt two.

Similarity 1:

Similarity 2:

Difference 1:

Difference 2:

(8)

10 Triads – Question 6

aims
- To understand the concept of triads.
- To identify the notes of a triad.
- To differentiate between major and minor triads.

Higher and Ordinary level.

Higher level Question 6 is worth **20 marks** (5% of the full exam). HL

Ordinary level Question 6 is worth **40 marks** (10% of the full exam).

exam TIPS

What you must do in answering Question 6:

1. You have to name the notes (usually three notes) asked for **in the order** in which they are printed in the bar/s. **DO NOT** arrange them into a triad unless asked to do so.

2. You must state the **tonality** (major/minor) of a triad, so you must therefore be able to identify the key of the piece. Spend time writing out the triad scale or chord box/grid (as in Question 8 – Harmony).

3. Higher level candidates usually then have to notate or identify this triad in the bass clef. Ordinary level candidates must identify the triad from a number of given triads.

4. Candidates must identify a certain number of bars in which the triad will fit the harmony of the named bars. (Work the answers out in a similar fashion to Question 8 – Harmony, Higher level.)

Description of triad chords

A **triad** chord consists of **three** different notes.
The root is the bottom (main) note of the chord and this is what we use to name the chord. When the root of the chord is at the bottom, all chord notes are stacked from this note upwards either on consecutive lines or in consecutive spaces.

Example: **C major triad**

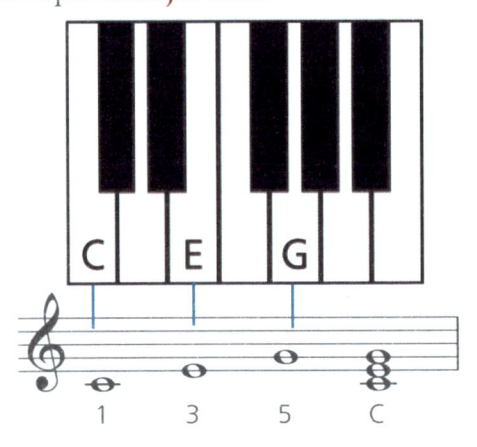

> **key point**
> The major triad is formed by the tonic (root or 1st note), 3rd and 5th note of the major scale that starts on the root. For example, the C major triad is formed by the notes C, E and G.

> **exam focus**
> In Junior Certificate Music you only have to know **major** and **minor** triads.

There are four types of triad chords:

- major
- minor
- diminished
- augmented

Basic triads in a major key

The chords are numbered using Roman numerals from I (= 1) to vii (= 7).

- To find all the basic chords in a key, build a simple triad (as above) on each note of the scale. You'll find that although the chords change from one key to the next, the pattern of major and minor chords is always the same.
- In a major key the chords ii and vi are minor chords and need a 'm' sign after the chord name to identify it correctly. Example: in the key of C major, chord ii is dm = D minor.
- Usually capital Roman numerals are used for major chords and small Roman numerals for minor chords.
- In a major key, the chords built on the first, fourth and fifth degrees of the scale are always major chords (I, IV and V). The chords built on the second, third and sixth degrees of the scale are always minor chords (ii, iii and vi). And the chord built on the seventh degree of the scale is a diminished chord. (You don't need to use chords iii and vi in Junior Certificate.)

> **key point**
> You must know the proper titles for the names of the degrees of the scale and of their relevant chords:
>
> **MAJOR KEY**
> I = Tonic = Doh
> ii = Supertonic = Re
> iii = Mediant = Mi
> IV = Subdominant = Fah
> V = Dominant = Soh
> vi = Submediant = La
> vii = Leading note = Ti

TRIADS – QUESTION 6   111

Modulation

Sometimes a piece of music moves into a new key. This is called **modulation**. It is very common in traditional classical music; longer movements almost always spend at least some time in a different key (usually a key closely *related to the main key*, such as the **dominant** or the **relative minor** or **relative major**).

HIGHER LEVEL QUESTION 6, 2010

Question 6: Triads (20 marks)
The verse below, played ONCE only.
This is the last piece you will hear on the recording.
Answer A, B, C and D.

Believe Me If All Those Endearing Young Charms

Believe Me If All Those Endearing Young Charms
THOMAS MOORE

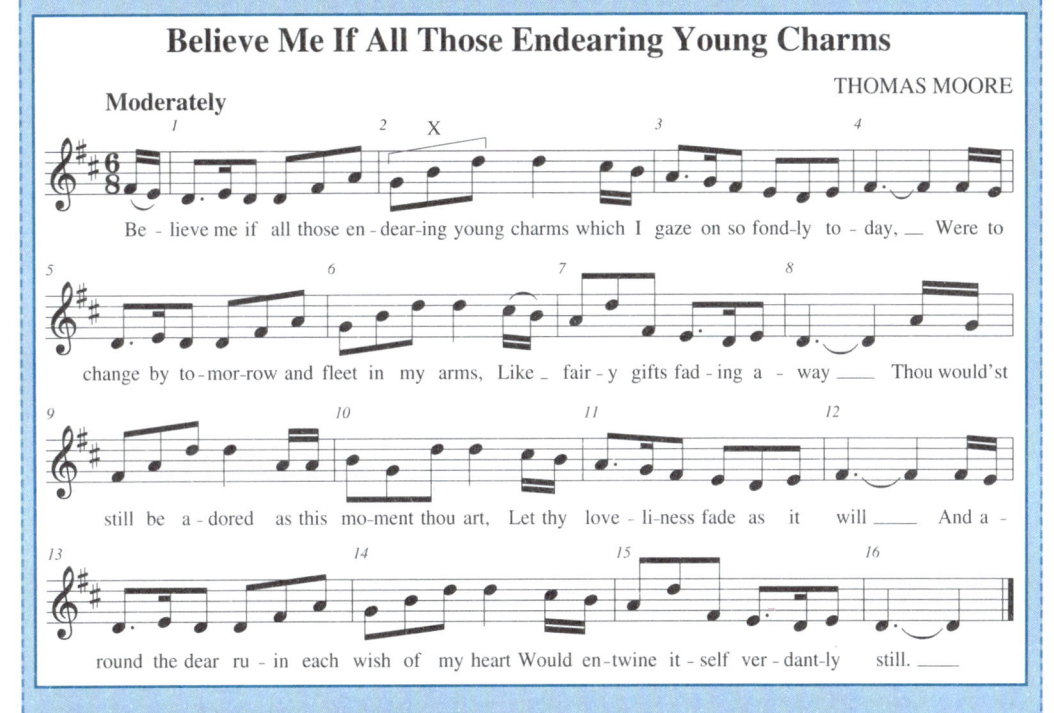

A What are the LETTER NAMES of the three notes at X (bar 2)?

_____

_____

_____

(6)

B These notes form the triad of

- D major
- E minor
- G major
- B minor

(4)

C This triad, printed on the BASS stave, is

(5)

D Select <u>one</u> of the following bars where this triad fits the melody.

- bar 3
- bar 8
- bar 9
- bar 10

(5)

11 Melody Writing – Question 7

aims
- To develop a confident approach to melody writing.
- To help minimise possible errors and omissions.

Higher and Ordinary level.

Answer **one** melody composition question: Question 7a **or** 7b **or** 7c.

exam focus
- Very few candidates attempt to answer Question 7a (setting a poem to music); this is generally not a very well answered question. Most candidates answer Question 7b or 7c quite well.
- Use a sharp B type pencil and be as neat as possible in your notation.

- Identify which question you want to answer.
- Study the given phrase (Question 7a, 7c) or bar (Question 7b) and decide what is most suitable for this melody.
- Check both the key signature **and** the given phrase to decide the tonic key (be aware of the harmony of the given bar/s and look out for any accidentals, which may mean the piece is in a **minor** key).
- Write out your triad scale for this key (or solfa).
- Check the clef to make sure it's the treble clef!

You may want to use the rough work manuscript before transferring the final melody. In either case, double check every bar of your answer when you have finished.

exam TIPS

1 Draw out your bar lines, double bar, clef and key signature, if needed.

2 Try to keep four bars of music to each line of stave, as in the given music of Question 7a or 7c.

3 You could number each bar, or number the first bar on each stave.

4 Be careful of upbeats (anacrusis). With an upbeat melody, remember to subtract that value in the final bar from the time signature.

5 Whether using tonic solfa or plotting chords, fill in the final cadence (probably a V– I **perfect** cadence).

6 If writing a melody plotting chords, insert chord names lightly over each bar so you won't forget.

7 Example, Question 7b: given bar 1/chord I, bar 2/chords ii, IV or vi, bar 3/chord V and finally end on a longer note on doh in bar 4 (chord I).

8 Plot out the rhythm for the full piece and **double check** your rhythmic values for every bar when you have finished.

In **Question 7a** (setting text to music), the rhythm and structure of your melody must come from the word setting and the syllable structure. Read through (in your head) the given text (poem) many times before you decide on your time signature and then on your rhythmic/syllabic structure. Don't forget to write the lyrics (words) under the correct notes.

In **Question 7b**, try to imagine what a musical **sequence** of bar 1 might sound like in bar 2 – it can work, but be careful that the sequence makes melodic sense. You might also develop the rhythm of bar 1 in bar 2. Do **not** use rhythmic ideas that are completely out of style with the melody of bar 1. Bar 3 should be the climax to the short phrase and therefore you should extend the range of the music upwards.

In **Question 7c**, when composing an answering phrase to the given four bars you could **develop** some of the material from the given phrase (rhythmic or melodic ideas; or add a sequence based on a development from this material). This reinforces the structure of the overall eight-bar melody. You will get NO marks for copying exactly from the given material. In all melody questions, try to use a **wide range** of over one octave (up to an octave and a half if possible).

Fill in the phrase marks (or breathing commas) over the phrase(s). Your melody must be musically interesting to gain high marks.

> **key point**
>
> In all melody questions **don't forget** to:
> - add a phrase mark.
> - end on doh.

MELODY WRITING – QUESTION 7

Common errors in Question 7

- Exact repetition of given material or material that is much too similar in rhythm or melody notes. **No marks** will be given for this.
- Inaccurate notes.
- No feeling of phrase or structure.
- Poor layout and messy notation (especially when written in pen and scribbled out).
- Missing phrase marks (commas).
- Not ending on the doh note; ending on the start note instead.

Marking Scheme

This is taken from the 2006 Marking Scheme – Higher level (SEC).

In **assessing melodies**, the correctors take the following into consideration:

- Continuation matches and carries on logically.
- Type of movement and shape and range.
- Patterns and intervals and approach to cadence(s).
- Balance and relationship to given opening.
- Climax (high note) or anti-climax (low note).
- Element of surprise or originality.
- For each repeating bar, drop down a band.

Four marks for **ending on doh** and **four marks** for writing in **phrase mark(s)**.
So the remaining 27 marks – melody (18), and rhythm (9) – are distributed as follows:

Band	Description	Marks
1	Excellent melodic style, convincing rhythm	24–27
2	Good shape and sense of direction, nearly matching rhythm	20–23
3	Careful melody, accurate rhythm	16–19
4	Some melodic interest, fairly accurate rhythm	12–15
5	No sense of key, inconsistent rhythm	8–11
6	Erratic shape in melody, weak rhythm	4–7
7	Little or no attempt	0–3

HIGHER LEVEL QUESTION 7, 2008

Question 7: Melodies (35 marks)
Answer ONE of the following - **A** or **B** or **C**.

A A phrase set to a given text

Here are four lines from 'The Rime of the Ancient Mariner'

> The western wave was all a-flame.
> The day was well nigh done!
> Almost upon the western wave
> Rested the broad bright sun.
>   Samuel Taylor Coleridge

- The first two lines have been set to music below.
- Compose your own FOUR-BAR phrase to complete the melody. Make your answering phrase **different** from the opening phrase.
- Use the following guidelines:
  1. Write a RHYTHM pattern to match the remaining words of the verse.
  2. Add suitable MELODY notes in the key of F for this rhythm.   (27)
  3. End on the KEYNOTE, that is, DOH.   (4)
  4. Insert the words or syllables underneath the correct notes.   (4)

At a walking pace *(Andante)*

The west-ern wave was _ all a - flame. The _ day was well nigh done!

Rhythm

Melody

OR

MELODY WRITING – QUESTION 7

B A phrase set to a given opening
Study this opening.

Rhythm

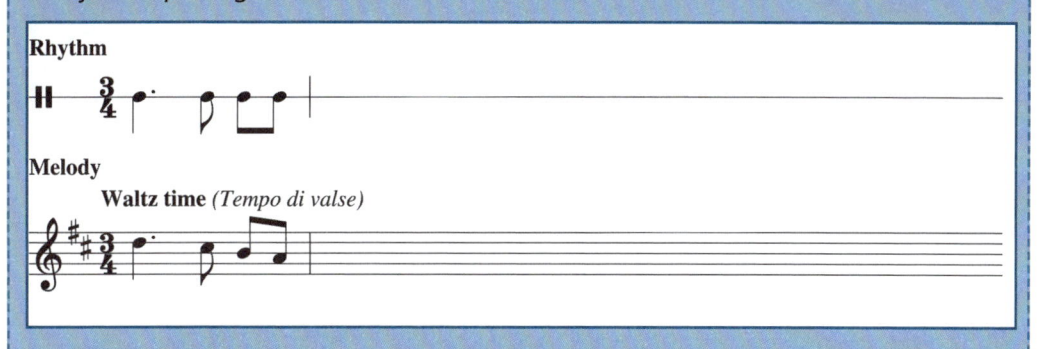

Melody
Waltz time (Tempo di valse)

Now complete this melody above as follows:
1. Add THREE bars to the given rhythm pattern.
2. Compose a MELODY in the key of D for this rhythm. (27)
3. End on the KEYNOTE, that is, DOH. (4)
4. Add suitable PHRASING. (4)

OR

C An answering phrase
Study this four-bar opening phrase.

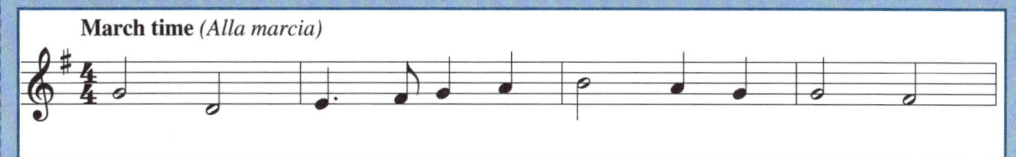

March time (Alla marcia)

Rhythm

Melody

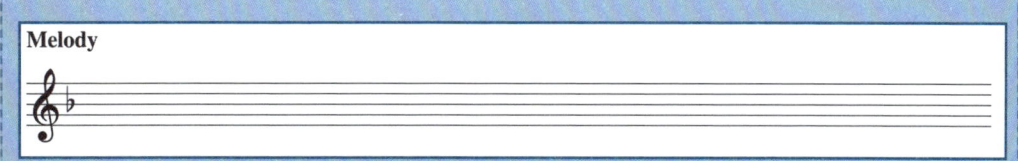

Now compose an *answering* phrase above to complete this melody.

Make your answering phrase different from the opening phrase, as follows:
1. Write a FOUR-BAR rhythm pattern.
2. Compose a MELODY in the key of G for this rhythm. (27)
3. End on the KEYNOTE, that is, DOH. (4)
4. Add suitable PHRASING. (4)

12 Harmony – Question 8

Note: Chapter 12 is for Higher level students **only** (45 marks).

aims
- To understand the concepts of harmony, cadences and chord structures.
- To enable you to approach this question with confidence.

Higher level candidates must answer **ONE** out of Questions 8a, 8b and 8c.

- Question 8a: composing melody and bass of cadences.
- Question 8b: SATB, four-part composition of cadences.
- Question 8c: composing backing chords for the given melody.

key point

Harmony is the relationship of any notes that happen at the same time. A chord is two or more notes played at the same time to produce harmony.

exam focus

The most popular choice is **Question 8c (backing chords)**, because if you understand how to answer Question 6 (triads), you should be able to answer Question 8c – once you know your cadences!

Cadences

A cadence is a place in a piece of music that feels like a stopping or resting point – the end of a musical phrase, like a comma or full stop in an English sentence. It is made up of two chords (sometimes with an approach chord). There are four types of cadences depending on what chord progressions are used.

Most pieces of music use regular phrases with cadences in a 4-, 8-, 16- or 32-bar pattern. Changes in the rhythm of a piece, like a pause in the rhythm or a lengthening of the note values, are often found at cadence points.

key point

When trying to identify cadences from a listening extract, ask yourself:
1. Does it sound finished or unfinished?
2. Does it end on a major or minor chord?
3. Is it a strong ending or a weak ending?

HARMONY – QUESTION 8

Name	Major Key	Minor Key
Perfect Cadence Strong final sound	V–I Use at end of a piece	V–i Chord V always has accidental in minor key
Plagal Cadence Sounds like *A-men* at the end of a hymn	IV–I Can also be used at end of a piece	iv–I Minor to minor
Imperfect Cadence Ends on dominant chord	I or ii or IV–V Q8c: at end of bar 4	I or iv–V
Interrupted Cadence Tonality change: unexpected sound	V–vi Major to minor chord in a major key	V–VI Minor to major chord in a minor key

key point

- The most commonly used triads form major chords and minor chords.
- If the interval between the root and the third of the chord is a **major third** the triad is a **major chord**.
- If the interval between the root and the third of the chord is a **minor third** then the triad is a **minor chord**.

Question 8 is worth 45 marks, or 15% of the written exam. It is vital that you:

- Understand how to identify the key and tonality.
- Can fill out a chord box/grid or triad scale in the key of your question.
- Understand, identify and compose cadence points.
- Can harmonise melodies with the correct backing chords (and cadence chords) in the correct manner (Question 8c).
- Understand how to compose for SATB using the rules of four-part writing (Question 8b).
- Can compose in the bass clef (Question 8a and 8b).
- Use a sharp B pencil and be as neat as possible in your notation.
- Double check every bar of your answer when you have finished.

In the exam:

- Identify which question you want to answer.
- Study the given material in each question.
- Study the question carefully to check the tonic key.
- Plot your chords in the chord box and/or write out your triad scale for this key.
- Don't forget: you need an *m* sign for a minor chord if using chord symbols (chords ii and vi are minor in a major key and chords i and iv are minor in a minor key).
- In a key with flats or sharps, you *must* use the flat or sharp symbol beside the chord name if needed.
- You do **NOT** need to add: tempo or dynamic markings; expression markings; phrasing and/or articulation.
- You do **NOT** need to use chord iii and chord vii.

Typical Marking Scheme

Question 8a: Melody and bass notes

X: imperfect cadence (IV–V) – 12 marks
Y: interrupted cadence (V–vi) – 12 marks
Z: perfect cadence and approach chord (ii–V–I) – 21
Total: 45 marks

Notes:
- Award marks for note accuracy.
- Awkward progressions: maximum deduction = 2 marks per cadence.
- Incorrect rhythmic values: no deduction.
- Inappropriate use of second inversion: deduct 2 marks.

Question 8b: SATB four-part writing

X: imperfect cadence (IV–V) – 12 marks
Y: interrupted cadence (V–vi) – 12 marks
Z: perfect cadence and approach chord (ii–V–I) – 21
Total: 45 marks

Notes:
- Award marks for note accuracy.
- Minor grammatical errors, e.g. spacing, double third (major chord), parallel.
- Fifths and octaves, leading note incorrectly used: maximum deduction = 1 mark per chord.
- Incorrect rhythmic values: no deduction.
- Inappropriate use of second inversion: deduct 2 marks.

HARMONY – QUESTION 8

Question 8c: Backing chords
Nine backing chords: 5 marks each.
Total: 45 marks

Notes:
- No chord symbol may be repeated twice in succession.
- The last two chords must be as indicated (cadence point).
- Accept lower-case letters for minor chords ONLY if there are capitals for major.
- Roman numerals: 0 marks.
- Incorrect notation (e.g. B for B flat, G for G minor) – allow only 2 marks out of 5 marks.

key point
Don't forget the cadences at the end of the first phrase and the final bars!

Rules for Question 8b: SATB four-part writing

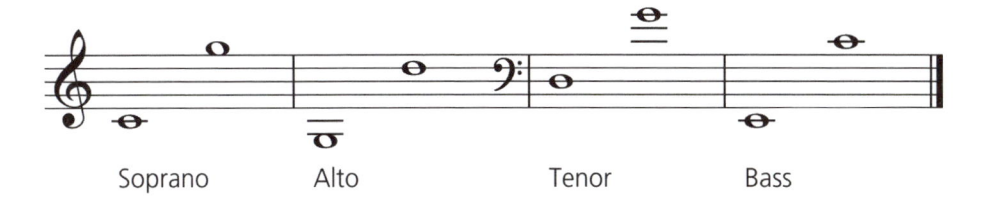

Soprano   Alto   Tenor   Bass

1. Keep each voice within its standard range.

2. Keep the upper three parts (S A T) smooth. Maintain common notes wherever possible. Stepwise motion is excellent. Where necessary, skips (interval jumps) should be as small as possible. Larger leaps (fourth, fifth and sixth) should be followed immediately by a return in the opposite direction. Avoid leaps of a seventh or greater than an octave. Bass voice may skip around more.
   Special Notes: Leading note (ti, seventh) should resolve up by step to the tonic (doh) when in an outer voice. Sharpened notes should resolve upward by step, and flatted notes should resolve downward by step in the same voice.

3. **Doubling with root position chords**
   Always try to double the bass (root), if possible. Never double the leading note. Occasionally you can omit the fifth, but **NEVER** double the third in a major chord.

4. **Spacing**
   Avoid voice crossing – keep voices in their normal order from highest to lowest pitches: S A T B. Always keep an octave or less between soprano/alto and between alto/tenor.

5. Chord structure
Try to maintain the same structure between adjacent chords unless other problems occur.

6. Outer voices (soprano/bass)
Have them move in contrary motion with each other as much as possible. Leading note should resolve up by step to tonic when in the soprano or bass.

7. Perfect intervals (1, 5 and 8)
Parallel (or consecutive) perfect fifths, octaves and unisons are **STRICTLY FORBIDDEN!**

8. Voice overlap
Avoid voice overlap – do not allow one voice to go beyond the previous note in an adjacent voice.

9. When bass notes are a second apart at cadences (e.g. IV–V):
Try to maintain the same structure in both chords.
Move the upper three voices in contrary motion to the bass.

10. When bass notes are a third apart (approaching cadence chords) (e.g. vi–IV–V):
Try to maintain the same structure.
Keep the two common tones in the same voice and move the remaining voice stepwise to the nearest chord note.

11. When bass notes are a fifth apart (e.g. V–I):
Try to maintain the same structure.
Keep the one common tone and move the other voices stepwise to the nearest chord notes. If a common note cannot be maintained, then move the upper three voices in the same direction (similar motion) to the nearest chord notes.

12. An Important Exception: The Interrupted Cadence
With V to vi (in major keys) and V to VI (in minor keys), when the leading note must resolve up to tonic, double the third of the vi (or VI) chord to avoid parallel fifths and/or octaves.

key point
Remember: practice makes perfect!

HARMONY – QUESTION 8

C Major Triads

C	dm	em	F	G7	am	bdim
I	ii	iii	IV	V7	vi	vii

G Major Triads

G	am	bm	C	D7	em	f#dim
I	ii	iii	IV	V7	vi	vii

D Major Triads

D	em	f#m	G	A7	bm	c#dim
I	ii	iii	IV	V7	vi	vii

A Major Triads

A	bm	c#m	D	E7	f#m	g#dim
I	ii	iii	IV	V7	vi	vii

E Major Triads

E	f#m	g#m	A	B7	c#m	d#dim
I	ii	iii	IV	V7	vi	vii

F Major Triads

F	gm	am	B♭	C7	dm	edim
I	ii	iii	IV	V7	vi	vii

B♭ Major Triads

B♭	cm	dm	E♭	F7	gm	adim
I	ii	iii	IV	V7	vi	vii

E♭ Major Triads

E♭	fm	gm	A♭	B♭7	cm	ddim
I	ii	iii	IV	V7	vi	vii

HIGHER LEVEL QUESTION 8, 2009

Question 8: Chord Progression (45 marks)

Answer ONE of the following: A or B or C.

A A melody and bass notes at cadences for keyboard
Study the following incomplete piece and then answer the questions below.

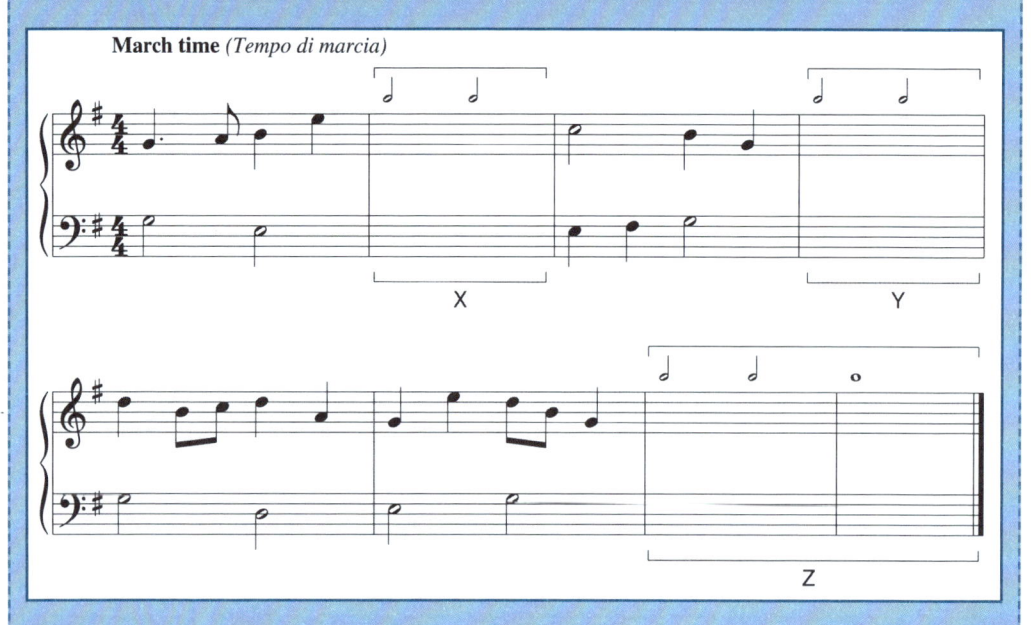

Add melody and bass notes to form the following:
1. At X, an IMPERFECT cadence (IV—V) (12)
2. At Y, an INTERRUPTED cadence (V—vi) (12)
3. At Z, a PERFECT cadence and its approach chord (ii—V—I) (21)

OR

B Chords at cadences for SATB choir
Study the following incomplete piece and then answer the questions below.

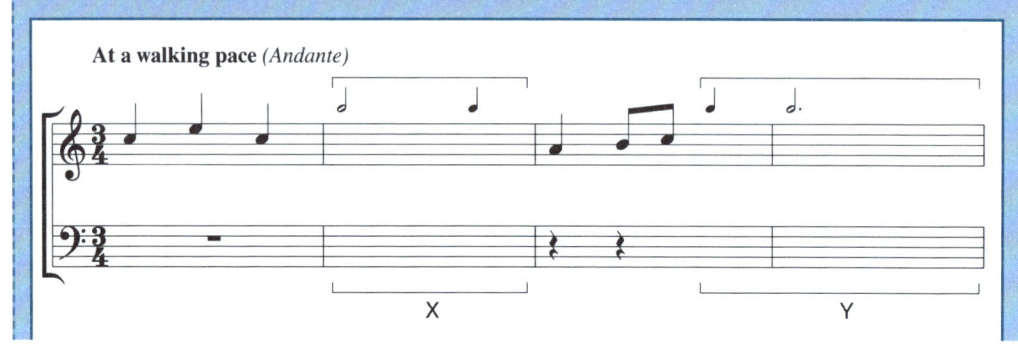

HARMONY – QUESTION 8

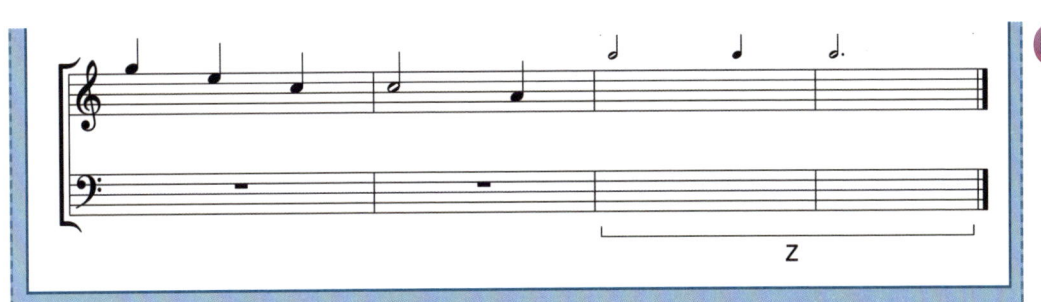

Add parts for three or four voices, as appropriate, to form the following:
1. At X, a PLAGAL cadence (IV—I) (12)
2. At Y, an IMPERFECT cadence (ii—V) (12)
3. At Z, a PERFECT cadence and its approach chord (IV—V—I) (21)

OR

C Backing chords
Study the following tune. It is intended for chordal accompaniment.

A-roving

Lively — Sea shanty

G

A - rov - ing, a - rov - ing, since rov-ing's been my ruin, ___ I'll go no more a - rov - ing with you fair maid.

The first symbol above the music indicates the chord of G.
Now fill in the other boxes as follows:
1. Select a suitable symbol as a backing chord in each box.
2. Do NOT use Roman numerals (for example, I, ii, IV, etc.)
3. Do NOT have the same symbol twice in succession.

(5 x 9 = 45)

13 Free Composition – Question 9

Note: This chapter is for Higher level students **only** (100 marks).

aims
- To write an original composition for voice or instrument(s) using a text.

exam focus
Very few candidates, if any, attempt this question!

This question is to be attempted by those candidates **NOT** answering Questions 6, 7 and 8.

Do **NOT** attempt this question unless you have been prepared for it and have agreed with your teacher that you can do this composition question instead of the triad, melody writing and harmony questions.

Very few candidates, if any, attempt this question each year!

There are **TWO** choices for writing an original composition in this question:

> **1** Composing a song or vocal work based on one of the three given verses; or
>
> **2** Composing an instrumental work illustrating a mood, based on one of the given verses.

For a vocal work, you must compose for voice/s **and** accompanying instrument/s, naming them appropriately on the score.

If composing a short piece for instrument/s you must remember to name which text you are using and name the mood that you wish to portray.

In either case the following compositional rules are essential:

- Read the text of the given verse carefully and a number of times before deciding on **instrumentation**.
- Think about the instruments that you will compose for, either as solo (flute, recorder or violin – non-transposing instruments) or as accompaniment: piano, guitar and harp are the most typical for accompaniment. Keep the accompaniment very simple.

FREE COMPOSITION – QUESTION 9

- Decide on the voice type and range for your vocalist/s. You could always compose for more than one vocalist.
- Decide on **tempo**, **metre** and **tonality**.
- Decide on musical **structure**, phrasing and cadential points (points of rest) and in what **key** you wish to compose your piece.
- You may want to plan out your **chord progression** or backing chords before you start composing your melody or rhythmic patterns. This will help keep your melody in a usual musical structure. Remember to compose some **counterpoint** (a descant or imitation) between instruments such as flute and violin.
- **Dynamics** and **articulation** are needed for instrumental composition.

For a **vocal work/song**: be careful when working out the rhythm of the lyrics and syllables that you are in the correct time signature.

- Keep the rhythm simple.
- Try to spot where you might use **word painting**, for example melismas or short accented notes to convey a particularly important word.
- Compose a melody and try to add sequences.
- The melody must be musically interesting, so try to compose a **climax** near the end of the piece.
- Don't forget to add **dynamics** in both parts. Dynamics in vocal music go above the staff.
- Be as neat as possible – use a sharp B pencil.

HIGHER LEVEL QUESTION 9, 2010

Question 9: Free Composition (100 marks)
NB: For candidates not selecting questions 6, 7 and 8 only.
Answer A or B.

A
1. Set ONE of the verses (i) or (ii) or (iii) below to your own original music.
2. Write for voice (or voices) and accompanying instrument (or instruments) of your choice.
3. Name these voices and instruments on the score. (100)

OR

B
1. Compose a short piece that will illustrate the mood of ONE of the verses below.
2. Name the instrument (or instruments) you select on the score.

(i) The Road Not Taken
    Two roads diverged in a yellow wood,
    And sorry I could not travel both
    And be one traveler, long I stood
    And looked down one as far as I could
    To where it bent in the undergrowth.
                        Robert Frost

(ii) Daybreak
    A wind came up out of the sea,
    And said, 'O mists, make room for me.'
    It hailed the ships, and cried, 'Sail on,
    Ye mariners, the night is gone.'
                        H. W. Longfellow

(iii) Na Coisithe
    I gcoim na hoíche cloisim iad,
    Na coisithe ar siúl;
    Airím iad, ní fheicim iad,
    Ní fios cá mbíonn a gcuaird.
                        Liam S. Gógáin

(100)

14 Chosen General Study – Question 8 OL / Question 10 HL

aims
- To explore in depth an area of music that is of personal interest to you.

Question 8 Ordinary level/Question 10 Higher level: **20 marks**.

Choose an area of study that interests you, for example:

- The musicals of Andrew Lloyd Webber.
- The development of jazz in the twentieth century.
- Pop music, from Abba to Westlife.
- English Madrigals of the Renaissance.

You need to be able to:

> 1. Name your study (pick a general title).
>
> 2. Name at least two pieces of music that you have listened to for your general study.
>
> 3. Name the performers/composers of those pieces.
>
> 4. Write an essay-type answer describing the background of this study area, why you chose this topic and, most important, some musical features (at least three) evident in the musical pieces you have named.
>
> 5. Be able to adapt your essay-type response to fully answer the question asked.

The syllabus states that all candidates must undertake a very general and **musically illustrated** study of **one** of the following topics:

> 1. **Day-to-day music.** Music that is commonly used and frequently heard in regular day-to-day experiences (e.g. liturgical and ritual music; music designed and used for advertising and marketing; music in the workplace; the use of music in restaurants and supermarkets; music as an accompaniment to physical exercises or as lullabies, etc.) leading towards an awareness of the differences between functional music and that produced for its own sake; **or**
>
> 2. Less obvious music from **early times**, i.e. medieval and Renaissance music; **or**
>
> 3. Less obvious music from **other places**, i.e. ethnic music other than Irish; **or**
>
> 4. **Art music** in modern times; **or**
>
> 5. Worthwhile **musical genres in the popular tradition**, including jazz.

exam focus

Don't forget to attempt this question. HL candidates: this question is the very last question on the paper. It is on the page after the Free Composition question (Question 9), which the huge majority of candidates do not and need not attempt. *So it is easily forgotten!*

Spend between 15 and 20 minutes on this question, depending on how fast you write. There is plenty of time allocated to Composition (Questions 6–8) and Chosen General Study after the CD excerpts are finished.

HIGHER LEVEL QUESTION 10, 2010

Question 10: General Study (20 marks)
Answer A, B and C.
Do NOT select pieces from your set songs, set works or Irish music here.

A Name your general study.
_____

To which category does this study belong?
_____

B List **two** pieces of music from your general study, with their composers or performers.

(i) Title: _____

Composer:
or
Performer: _____
(4)

(ii) Title: _____

Composer:
or
Performer: _____
(4)

C You are asked to write an article for a student magazine. Briefly introduce your general study and state why you find it interesting.
(3)

Name **three** musical features of your general study and briefly describe each one.

Musical feature 1: _____
Description: _____
(3)

Musical feature 2: _____
Description: _____
(3)

Musical feature 3: _____
Description: _____
(3)

ORDINARY LEVEL QUESTION 8, 2009

Question 8: General study (20 marks)
Answer A, B and C.
Do NOT include pieces from your set songs, set works or Irish music here.

A (i) Name your general study.
_____

(ii) To which category does it belong?
- day-to-day music.
- modern art music.
- the popular tradition.
- ethnic music (other than Irish).
- medieval and renaissance music.

_____
(2)

B Give the titles and name the composers or performers of <u>two</u> pieces of music under this heading.
(i) Title:
_____

Composer: _____
or
Performer: _____

(ii) Title:
_____

Composer: _____
or
Performer: _____
(8)

C Name <u>two</u> musical features of your general study, and write a brief note on each of them.
Choose, for example, instruments, voices, melodies, form, rhythm, musical style, harmony, mood.

Musical feature 1: _____
Brief note: _____
(5)

Musical feature 2: _____
Brief note: _____
(5)

15 Instruments of the Orchestra and Performing Mediums

aims
- To be able to identify the 'performing medium': a symphony orchestra, a string quartet, a jazz band, etc.
- To know what different instruments look and sound like.

The symphony orchestra

A **symphony orchestra** is a large orchestra, with up to 100 players, separated into their 'families' of instruments:

- strings.
- woodwind.
- brass.
- percussion.

The orchestra has a **conductor**, and the **leader** of the orchestra is usually the first violin player sitting nearest the conductor.

Usually the oboe player sounds the note A so that all the players can tune their instruments.

One example of a **symphony orchestra** is the National Symphony Orchestra (NSO), which is run in conjunction with RTÉ. A **concert orchestra** (e.g. the RTÉ Concert Orchestra) is a smaller orchestra and plays a wide variety of music from classical to popular.

A **chamber orchestra** is an even smaller orchestra. Most of the players are string players, and only a few woodwind or brass players are needed occasionally. Sometimes there is a conductor but often there is not, and the leader takes the role of bringing in the instruments and setting the tempo. The Irish Chamber Orchestra is an example of a superb chamber orchestra.

> **key point**
>
> **Chamber music** means music to be performed in a smaller hall or room, not in a large concert hall. It can include music for solo piano, accompanied singer or instrumentalist, **string quartet** (two violins, viola and cello), or any small group of players/singers.

Layout of the modern symphony orchestra

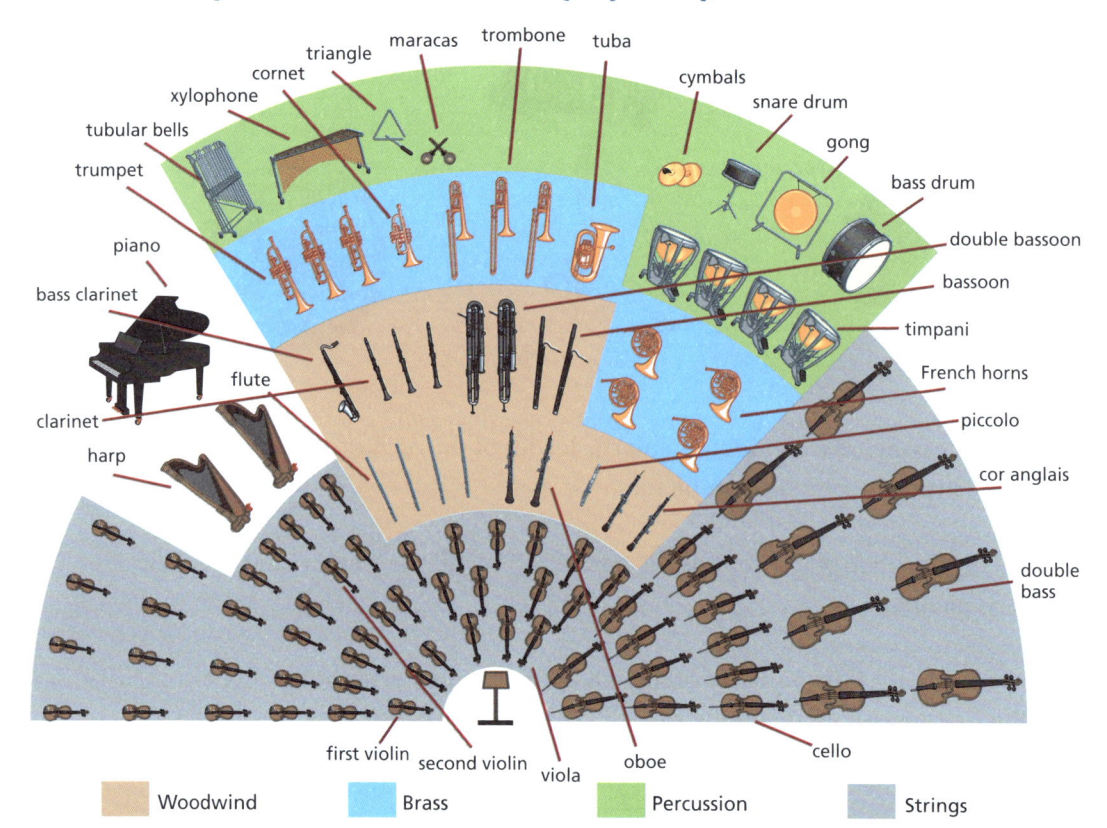

Labels: tubular bells, trumpet, xylophone, cornet, triangle, maracas, trombone, tuba, cymbals, snare drum, gong, bass drum, double bassoon, bassoon, timpani, French horns, piccolo, cor anglais, double bass, cello, oboe, viola, second violin, first violin, harp, clarinet, bass clarinet, piano, flute

Woodwind | Brass | Percussion | Strings

16 Structure and Forms of Music

aims
- To become familiar with the terminology associated with the structure and layout of a piece of music.

Aria. A solo vocal piece with instrumental or piano accompaniment.
Binary form. A way of structuring a piece of music into two sections (A and B), both of which are usually repeated.
Cantata. A musical composition, often using a sacred/religious text, comprising recitatives, arias, choruses and instrumental pieces.
Concerto (solo). A composition, typically in three movements, for an orchestra and one solo instrument.
Concerto grosso. A composition for a small group of instrumental soloists and an orchestra.
Da Capo is a musical term in Italian, which means 'from the beginning' (literally 'from the head'), often abbreviated to the letters **D.C.**
- **D. C. al Coda:** repeat from the beginning to an indicated place and then play the coda.
- **D. C. al Fine:** repeat from the beginning up to the word *fine*.

Dal Segno ('from the sign') (D.S.) is an instruction to repeat a passage starting from this symbol: 𝄋
- **D.S. al Coda:** repeat back to the symbol, and when you reach the coda symbol, jump to the section of music labelled the coda.
- **D.S. al Fine:** repeat back to the symbol, and end the piece at the bar marked *fine*.

Form is simply a concept used to describe the layout, structure and construction of a piece of music.
Lieder. German word meaning 'art song' (aria). A song that is usually part of a 'song cycle' or a collection of (romantic) songs.
Madrigal has two distinct, unconnected meanings: a poetic and musical form dating from fourteenth-century Italy; and a sixteenth- or seventeenth-century setting of secular verse.
Musical. A form of popular theatre. It developed from comic opera at the end of the nineteenth century, and includes solos, choruses and instrumental pieces, usually with complex choreography. The most famous modern composers are Stephen Sondheim (*Sweeney Todd, Into the Woods*), Andrew Lloyd Webber (*Evita, Phantom of the Opera*) and Stephen Schwartz (*Wicked, The Baker's Wife*), all of whose shows have been very successful on Broadway (in New York) and in the West End (London).
Opera. A musical theatrical presentation in which a dramatic performance is set to music and involving soloists and chorus, example, Bizet's *Carmen* or Puccini's *La Bohéme*.
Oratorio. A musical composition for voices and orchestra, usually telling a religious story in a concert setting without costumes, scenery or dramatic action. Example, Handel's Messiah.
Overture. The instrumental introduction to an opera, musical, oratorio or even a large instrumental work. An overture (*symphonic poem*) can also be a free-standing large-scale instrumental piece of *programme music*.
Plainchant. Monophonic unison chant, originally unaccompanied, of the Christian liturgies.
Ritornello. The 'returning' music (i.e. the main theme or refrain).
Ritornello form. A form in which the main theme (the ritornello) keeps returning. *Episodes* (contrasting new music or material) occur between the recurrences of the main tune.

Sonata. Usually a piece in three movements for keyboard (e.g. piano sonata), or for keyboard and one other instrument (e.g. violin sonata).

Sonata Form. The form of a single movement in a type of large ABA (ternary form) structure. The main sections of this form are the **exposition** (tonic key – dominant key), the **development** (many modulations) and the **recapitulation** (tonic key).

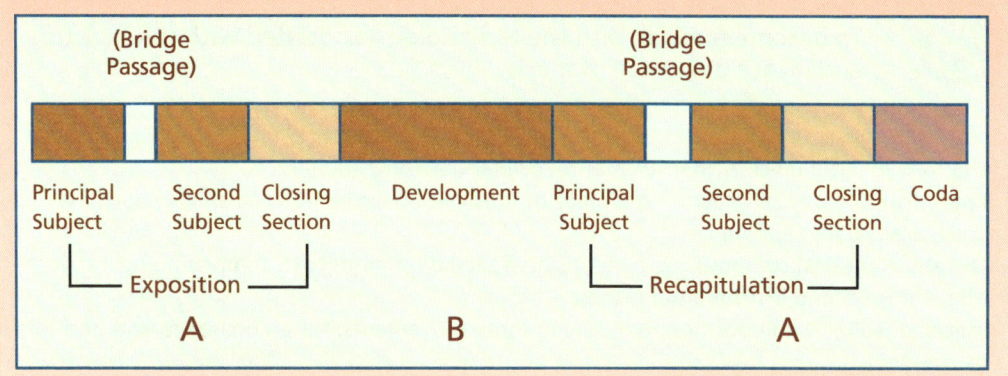

(Bridge Passage)		(Bridge Passage)	
Principal Subject	Second Subject	Closing Section	Development	Principal Subject	Second Subject	Closing Section	Coda
└── Exposition ──┘		└── Recapitulation ──┘	
A	B	A	

Symphony. An extended piece in three or more movements for symphony orchestra, e.g. Beethoven's Fifth Symphony.

Ternary Form. A three-part structure. The first and third parts have similar music, while the second part contrasts in some way with the music of the first part. Ternary form is often represented as A B A (or A B A1).

FIRST SECTION	SECOND SECTION	FIRST SECTION

Rondo Form. Rondo Form is so called because one section returns again and again. As you can see in the diagram below, the first section of music alternates with the second and third sections, i.e. A B A C A B A.

FIRST SECTION	SECOND SECTION	FIRST SECTION	THIRD SECTION	FIRST SECTION	SECOND SECTION	FIRST SECTION

Theme and Variations Form. This consists of a theme and several variations, in which the main tune (theme) is elaborated, developed and transformed (by changing the rhythm, melody and harmony, tonality etc. of the main tune).

THEME	FIRST VARIATION	SECOND VARIATION	THIRD VARIATION	CODA

Glossary of Musical Terms

A capella – unaccompanied singing (by a group or soloist).
A niente – to nothing, e.g. to *ppp*.
A tempo – return to the previous tempo.
Absolute music – music composed purely for the sake of composition, with no story or illustrative purposes in mind. The opposite of programme music.
Accelerando, accel. – gradually becoming faster.
Accent – placed above a note to indicate stress or emphasis.
Accidental – a sharp, flat, or natural not included in the given key.
Accompaniment – a vocal or instrumental part that supports a solo part.
Ad libitum, ad lib – a term that permits the performer to extemporise or vary the music at will.
Adagio – slow: slower than andante, faster than largo.
Agitato – agitated; with excitement.
Al coda – to the coda.
Al fine – to the end.
Alla breve – cut time; metre in which there are two beats in each measure and a half note receives one beat.
Allargando, allarg. – slowing of tempo, usually with increasing volume; most frequently occurs toward the end of a piece.
Allegretto – a little slower than allegro.
Allegro – fast.
Alto – a female vocalist with a range between the soprano and tenor parts.
Alto clef – the C clef falling on the third line of the staff. Normally used by the viola.
Anacrusis – see *upbeat*.
Andante – at a walking pace.
Andantino – a little faster than andante.
Animato – animated; lively.
Antiphonal – alternating sounds; see *call and response*.
Appoggiatura – a non-chordal tone, usually a semitone or tone above the notated tone, which is performed on the beat and then resolved.
Arpeggio – the pitches of a chord sung or played one after the other, rather than simultaneously.
Atonality – lacking a tonal centre. Music that is written and performed without regard to any specific key.
Augmentation – compositional technique in which a melodic line is repeated in longer note values. The opposite of diminution.

Backbeat – beats 2 and 4 are accented, usually by a snare drum.
Bar line – the vertical line placed on the staff to divide the music into measures.
Bass clef – the other name for the F clef.
Bass – the lowest-pitched member of a family of instruments; lowest voice; lowest part in a musical composition.
Basso continuo, Continuo, Thorough-bass – the Baroque practice in which the bass part is played by a cello or bassoon while a keyboard instrument performs the bass line and the indicated chords (figured bass).
Bends – a guitar technique in which a note is altered in pitch by pushing the string up.
Binary form – a composition of two sections – A B – each of which may be repeated.
Bitonality – the occurrence of two different tonalities at the same time.
Brass family – wind instruments made out of metal with either a cup- or funnel-shaped mouthpiece, such as trumpet, cornet, bugle, flugelhorn, trombone, tuba, baritone horn, euphonium and French horn.
Broken chords – notes of a chord played in succession rather than simultaneously; see *arpeggio*.

C clef – a clef usually centred on the first line (soprano clef), third line (alto clef), fourth line (tenor clef), or third space (vocal tenor clef) of the staff. Wherever it is centred, that line or space becomes middle C.

Cadence – a chordal or melodic progression which occurs at the close of a phrase, section, or composition, giving a feeling of a temporary or permanent ending. The four cadences are perfect, plagal, imperfect and interrupted cadences (see Chapter 12).
Cadenza – a solo passage, often virtuosic, usually near the end of a piece, either written by the composer or improvised by the performer.
Call and response – a technique of African folk origin by which a solo singer is answered by a chorus singing a repeated phrase; see *antiphonal music*.
Canon – the strictest form of imitation, in which two or more parts have the same melody but start at different points.
Canonic – a term used to describe a polyphonic (counterpoint) style of music in which all the parts have the same melody but which start at different times.
Cantabile – in a singing style.
Cantata – Baroque sacred or secular choral composition containing solos, duets and choruses, with orchestral or continuo accompaniment.
Chamber music – music for a small ensemble.
Chorale – a hymn-like song, characterised by blocked chords.
Chord – a combination of two or more tones sounded simultaneously.
Chromatic scale – a scale composed of 12 semitones.
Classical – usually music composed during the period 1770–1820.
Clef – a symbol placed at the beginning of the staff to indicate the pitch of the notes on the staff. The most commonly used clefs in choral music are the G or treble clef, and the F or bass clef.
Coda – closing section of a composition. An added ending.
Coloratura – elaborate, ornamented vocal passage.
Common time – 4/4 metre.
Con – with.
Con brio – with spirit; vigorously.
Con moto – with motion.
Concert pitch – the international tuning pitch – currently the note is A 440 hertz. The pitch for non-transposing (C) instruments.

Concertino – the group of soloists in a *concerto grosso*.
Concerto – a piece for a soloist and orchestra.
Concerto grosso – a piece for a small ensemble of soloists and orchestra (*ripieno*).
Concordant (consonance) – a satisfied chord or interval; perfect intervals and major and minor thirds and sixths.
Conductor – the person who directs a group of musicians.
Conjunct – pitches on successive degrees of the scale; opposite of disjunct.
Continuo – see *basso continuo*.
Corda, corde – string. Una corda (one string) – in piano music, this means play with the soft (left) pedal.
Countermelody – a vocal part that contrasts with the main melody.
Counterpoint – the technique of combining single melodic lines or parts of equal importance (polyphonic texture).
Crescendo – gradually become louder.
Cut common time – 2/2 metre.

Da capo, D. C. – return to the beginning.
Dal segno, D. S. – repeat from the sign. Frequently followed by *al Fine*.
Diatonic – the notes of a key in a major or minor scale.
Diminished – an interval that has been decreased by one semitone.
Diminuendo, dim. – gradually become softer.
Diminution – the shortening of note values; the opposite of augmentation.
Disjunct – the term used to describe intervals larger than a second; the opposite of conjunct.
Dissonance (discordant) – unrestful sounds, e.g. intervals of seconds and sevenths; the opposite of consonance.
Distortion – a sound effect that overloads the speaker, used in rock and heavy metal.
Divisi, div – an indication of divided musical parts.
Dolce – sweetly.
Dolcissimo – very sweetly.
Dominant – the fifth degree of the major or minor scale. Also the term for the triad built on the fifth degree, labelled V in harmonic analysis.

GLOSSARY OF MUSICAL TERMS

Duet – a piece for two performers.
Duplet – a group of two notes performed in the time of three of the same kind.
Dynamics – varying degrees of loud and soft.

e – Italian word meaning 'and'.
Echo – often called a 'delay': a sound effect produced by a guitar pedal.
Embellishment – ornamentation.
Enharmonic – a term used to describe notes of the same pitch which have different names, e.g. C sharp and D flat.
Espressivo – expressively.

Falsetto – a style of male singing in which, by partial use of the vocal chords, the voice is able to reach the pitch of a female.
Feedback – used mainly by rock musicians to produce a high-pitched sound.
Fermata – hold; pause.
Finale – the last movement of a symphony or sonata, or the last selection of an opera.
Fine – the end.
Form – the design or structure of a musical composition.
Forte, *f* – loud.
Fortissimo, *ff* – very loud.
Fortississimo, *fff* – very, very loud.
Fugue – a contrapuntal compositional device like a canon.
fz – forzando or forzato. Synonymous with sforzando (*sf* or *sfz*).

Glissando, gliss. – sliding, by playing a rapid scale.
Grave – slow, solemn.
Grosso, grosse – great, large.

Harmony – the sounding of two or more simultaneous musical notes in a chord.
Hemiola – switching between metres 3/4 and 6/8.
Homophonic – musical texture characterised by a main melody and other accompaniment.
Hook – a memorable part of a popular song.

Imitation – compositional device involving much repetition by different voices/ instruments playing similar material at different times.

Improvisation – music to be invented by the performer on the spot in jazz.
Instrumentation – the art of composing, orchestrating, or arranging for an instrumental ensemble.
Interval – the distance between two pitches is the interval between them. The name of an interval depends both on how the notes are written and the actual distance between the notes as measured in semitones.
Intonation – a way of producing notes with regard to accurate pitch and tuning.
Inversion – turning a chord or a melodic pattern upside-down.

Key signature – the sharps or flats placed at the beginning of the staff to denote the scale on which the music is based.

Larghetto – slower than largo.
Largo, lento – slow.
Leading note – the seventh degree of the major scale.
Ledger lines – short lines placed above and below the staff for pitches beyond the range of the staff.
Legato – smooth, connected.
Libretto – a book of text containing the words of an opera.

Major chord – a triad composed of a root, major third, and perfect fifth.
Marcato – emphasised, heavily accented.
Medieval – the period before the Renaissance, c. 500–1450, marking the music of the early Christian church.
Melisma or **melismatic** – many notes written to one syllable.
Meno mosso – less motion.
Mezzo – half, medium.
Modal – scales that preceded the development of major and minor scales and tonality: gapped scale, whole tone scale, pentatonic scale.
Moderato – moderate speed.
Modulation – the process of changing from one key to another within a composition.
Molto – very; used with other terms, e.g. molto allegro.
Mosso – rapid. *Meno mosso*: less rapid. *Più mosso*: more rapid.

Motif – a short musical idea that occurs often in a piece of music. A short melodic idea may also be called a motiv, a motive, a cell, or a figure.
Moto – motion. *Con moto*: with motion.

Natural – a musical symbol that cancels a previous sharp or flat.
Non troppo – not too much. Used with other terms, e.g. *non troppo allegro*: not too fast.

Octave – the interval between the first and eighth notes of a scale.
Octet – a piece for eight instruments or voices.
Open fifth – a triad without a third.
Open strings – strings are not stopped, fingered, or fretted.
Opus, Op. – literally 'work'. Used to indicate the chronological order of a composer's works, e.g. Op. 1, Op. 2.
Orchestral music – music written for a large group of instruments. These usually include strings, brass, percussion and woodwind.
Orchestration – the art of writing, arranging or scoring for the orchestra.
Ornamentation – note or notes added to the original melodic line for embellishment, e.g. trills, mordents, turns or grace notes.
Ostinato – a repeated melodic or rhythmic pattern.
Ottava alta (8va) – play an octave higher.
Ottava bassa (8vb) – play an octave lower.
Overture – the introductory music for an opera, oratorio or ballet.

Passing notes – unaccented notes that move between two chordal notes to which they do not belong harmonically.
Pedal note – a long held note (usually tonic or dominant) over which various harmonies occur, producing harmonic tension.
Perfect – a term used to label fourth, fifth, and octave intervals. It corresponds to the major, as given to seconds, thirds, sixths, and sevenths.
Perfect cadence – the chordal progression of dominant to tonic: in a major key V–I; in a minor key V–i.
Perfect pitch – the ability to hear and identify a note without any other musical support.

Pesante – heavy.
Petite – little.
Peu a peu – little by little.
Phrase – a relatively short portion of a melodic line which expresses a musical idea, comparable to a line or sentence in poetry.
Pianissimo, *pp* – very soft.
Pianississimo, *ppp* – very, very soft; the softest common dynamic marking.
Piano, *p* – soft.
Pianoforte – literally 'soft-loud'. The full name for the piano. It has 88 keys.
Pitch – the highness or lowness of a note.
Più – more. Used with other terms, e.g. *più mosso*: more motion.
Pizzicato – plucked. On stringed instruments, plucking the string.
Plagal cadence – sometimes called the 'Amen' cadence. The chordal progression of subdominant to tonic: in a major key IV–I; in a minor key iv–i.
Poco – little. Used with other terms, e.g. *poco accel.*: a little faster; *poco a poco*: little by little.
Poco piu mosso – a little more motion.
Portamento – very smooth transition between two notes (nearly glissando-like).
Postlude – the final piece in a multi-movement work. Organ piece played at the end of a church service.
Prelude – an introductory movement or piece.
Premiere – first performance.
Prestissimo – very, very fast. The fastest tempo.
Presto – very fast.
Primo – first.
Programme music – music based on a story, mood or idea.
Prologue – an introductory piece that presents the background for an opera.

Quartet – a piece for four instruments or voices; four performers.
Quasi – almost. Used with other terms.
Quintet – a piece for five instruments or voices; five performers.

Rallentando, rall. – Gradually slower. Identical to *ritardando*.
Range – the notes, from lowest to highest, that an instrument is capable of producing.

GLOSSARY OF MUSICAL TERMS

Refrain – a short section of repeated material that occurs at the end of each stanza.
Register – a specific area of the range of an instrument.
Relative major and minor scales – major and minor scales which have the same key signature.
Repeat – the repetition of a section or a composition as indicated by particular signs.
Rest – a symbol used to denote silence.
Rhythm – the organisation of sound in time.
Riff – a repeated short phrase, like an ostinato, in a jazz composition.
Rimshot – when a drummer hits the rim of snare or side drum.
Rinforzando – a reinforced accent.
Ritardando, rit. – gradually becoming slower
Ritenuto – immediate reduction in tempo.
Ritmico – rhythmically.
Roll – on percussion instruments, a sticking technique consisting of a rapid succession of notes.
Romanticism – the period c. 1820–1900.
Root position – the arrangement of a chord in which the root is in the lowest voice.
Round – like a canon, a song in which two or more parts have the same melody but start at different points. The parts may be repeated as desired.
Rubato – flexibility of tempo to help achieve expressiveness.
Run – a rapid scale passage.
Rustico – pastoral, rustic, rural.

SATB – Soprano, Alto, Tenor, Bass.
Scale – a progression of notes in a stepwise motion in a specific order.
Score – the written depiction of all the parts of a musical ensemble with the parts stacked vertically and rhythmically aligned.
Secco – dry.
Semitone – a half step. The smallest interval on the keyboard.
Semplice – simple.
Sempre – always. Used with other terms, e.g. *sempre staccato*.
Senza (sans) – without. Used with other terms, e.g. *senza crescendo*.
Sequence – the repetition of a melodic pattern at a higher or lower pitch.

Seventh chord – when a seventh (above the root) is added to a triad (root, third, fifth), the result is a seventh chord, e.g. the dominant triad in the key of C major, g–b–d, with the added seventh becomes g–b–d–f and is labelled V^7.
Sforzando, *sfz*, *sf* – a sudden strong accent on a note or chord.
Sharp – a symbol (#) that raises the pitch of a note one-half step.
Simile – similar, an indication to continue in the same manner.
Six-four chord – the second inversion of a triad, made by placing the fifth of the chord in the lowest voice.
Slur – a curved line placed above or below two or more notes of different pitch to indicate that they are to be performed in legato style.
Solmisation – the term for using syllables for the degrees of the major scale: doh, re, mi, fah, soh, la, ti, do. The (natural) minor scale is la, ti, doh, re, mi, fah, soh, la.
Solo – performed alone or as the predominant part.
Sonata – a solo instrumental piece (sometimes with piano accompaniment), often in four movements.
Sostenuto – sustained.
Spiccato – on string instruments, a bowing technique wherein the bow is bounced on the string at moderate speed.
Staccato – detached sounds, indicated by a dot over or under a note. The opposite of legato.
Stretto – a contrapuntal compositional device where imitative parts quickly overlap.
Strophic – a song in which all the stanzas of the text are sung to the same music. The opposite of through-composed.
Subdominant – the fourth degree of the major or minor scale. Also the name of the triad built on the fourth degree of the scale, indicated by IV in a major key and by iv in a minor key.
Subito – suddenly.
Submediant – the sixth degree of a major or minor scale. Also the name of the triad built on the sixth degree of the scale, indicated by VI in a major key and by vi in a minor key.

Sul – on the …
Supertonic – the second degree of the major or minor scale. Also the name of the triad built on the second degree of the scale, indicated by II in a major scale and ii in a minor scale.
Sur – on, over.
Suspension – The use of a non-chord note to delay the resolution of a chord, frequently as it occurs in a cadence.
Syllabic – one note per syllable.
Symphony – a piece for large orchestra, usually in four movements, in which the first movement is often in sonata form. A large orchestra.
Syncopation – accent on an off beat.

Tanto – much, so much.
Tempo – the rate of speed in a musical work.
Tempo primo – return to the original tempo.
Tenor – high male voice, between the alto and baritone parts.
Tenuto (*ten.*) – hold or sustain a note longer than the indicated value.
Ternary form – three-part form in which the middle section is different from the other sections. Indicated by A B A.
Terraced dynamics – the Baroque style of using sudden changes in dynamic levels, as opposed to gradual increase and decrease in volume.
Tessitura – the comfortable pitch range of a vocal part.
Texture – the term used to describe the way in which melodic lines are combined, either with or without accompaniment. Types include monophonic, homophonic and polyphonic (contrapuntal).
Theme – a longer section of melody that keeps reappearing in the music. Themes generally are at least one phrase long and often have several phrases. Many longer works of music, such as symphony movements, have more than one melodic theme.
Theme and variations – a statement of musical subject followed by restatements in different guises.
Thorough-bass – *see* **basso continuo**.
Through-composed – a term used to describe a song in which the music for each stanza is different. The opposite of strophic.

Tie – a curved line over or below two or more notes of the same pitch. The first pitch is sung or played and held for the duration of the notes affected by the tie.
Timbre – tone colour or quality of an instrument's sound.
Time signature – see Chapter 4.
Tonality – the term used to describe the organisation of the melodic and harmonic elements to give a feeling of a key centre or a tonic pitch.
Tone – sound that has a definite pitch. Any given tone is characterised by length, loudness, timbre and a characteristic pattern of attack and fade.
Tonic – the first note of a key. Also the name of the chord built on the first degree of the scale, indicated by I in a major key and i in a minor key.
Tranquillo – tranquilly; quietly; calmly.
Transposition – changing the key of a composition.
Treble clef – the G clef falling on the second line of the staff.
Treble – the highest instrument part. A boy soprano.
Triad – a chord of three tones arranged in thirds, e.g. the C major triad c–e–g, root–third–fifth.
Trill (*tr.*) – a musical ornament performed by the rapid alternation of a given note with a major or minor second above.
Triplet – a group of three notes performed in the time of two of the same kind.
Tritone – a chord comprised of three whole tones resulting in an augmented fourth or diminished fifth.
Troppo – Too much. Used with other terms, e.g. *allegro non troppo*, not too fast.
Tutti – all. A direction for the entire ensemble to sing or play simultaneously.
Twelve-tone technique (serial music) – a system of composition which uses the twelve tones of the chromatic scale in an arbitrary arrangement called a tone row or series. The row may be used in its original form, in its inversion, in retrograde, and in the inversion of the retrograde. The system was devised by Arnold Schoenberg in the early twentieth century.

GLOSSARY OF MUSICAL TERMS

Un peu – a little. Used with other terms, e.g. *un peu piano*.
Un poco – a little.
Una corda – soft pedal (left pedal on piano).
Unison – singing or playing of the same notes by all singers or players, either at exactly the same pitch or in a different octave.
Upbeat (anacrusis) – one or more notes occurring before the first bar line.

V.S. or **volti subito** – turn (the page) quickly.

Variation – the development of a theme by the use of melodic, rhythmic and harmonic changes.
Vibrato – repeated fluctuation of pitch.
Virtuoso – a brilliant, skilful performer.
Vivace – lively, brisk, quick, bright.
Vivo – lively, bright.

Woodwind family – instruments, originally made of wood, in which sound is produced by the vibration of air, including recorders, flutes, clarinets, saxophones, oboes, cor anglais and bassoons.